"Nothing would ha   t
the words of the tit   ...th
John Stott, not just reading John Stott on the Bible. For in his preaching
as in his writing, John Stott's greatest gift was to help people see and
hear clearly what the Bible itself actually says, and then, of course, to
challenge us as to how we should respond to what we see and hear. Not
all of us possess the complete works of John Stott. But we do possess
the complete Bible. These sensitively edited extracts from Stott's
writings will not only introduce new readers to the riches of his biblical
exposition (and make them hungry for more), but will surely also introduce them to riches of God's word they had not seen before."

Christopher J. H. Wright, international ministries director,
Langham Partnership

"No one I have known has loved, preached, taught and lived the Bible
any more than John Stott. He often quoted Spurgeon's comment that
we should seek for our very blood to become 'Bibline'; so seriously
should we soak in Scripture in order to know and live it. This new series
will give us daily help in just such living."

Mark Labberton, president, Fuller Theological Seminary, author of *Called*

"More than any other author, John Stott urges us to engage in double
listening. He wants us to listen to the Word God spoke and the world
God loves so that we apply the timeless truths of Scripture to the ever-
changing context of our life. To help us, he explains the Bible with
clarity, charity and humility. His writings propel us to Jesus and into
the mission of God in the world."

Greg Jao, vice president and director of campus engagement,
InterVarsity Christian Fellowship

READING
ROMANS

with

JOHN STOTT

VOLUME
1

WITH QUESTIONS FOR

GROUPS OR INDIVIDUALS

JOHN STOTT

with DALE & SANDY LARSEN

IVP Connect

An imprint of InterVarsity Press
Downers Grove, Illinois

InterVarsity Press
P.O. Box 1400, Downers Grove, IL 60515-1426
ivpress.com
email@ivpress.com

This volume is abridged and edited from The Message of Romans *©1994 by John R. W. Stott, originally published under the title* Romans: God's Good News for the World, *by permission of Inter-Varsity Press, England. Some of the discussion questions are from* Romans: Encountering the Gospel's Power *©1998 by John R. W. Stott, originally published by InterVarsity Press, Downers Grove, Illinois, USA.*

InterVarsity Press® is the book-publishing division of InterVarsity Christian Fellowship/USA®, a movement of students and faculty active on campus at hundreds of universities, colleges and schools of nursing in the United States of America, and a member movement of the International Fellowship of Evangelical Students. For information about local and regional activities, visit intervarsity.org.

Cover design: Cindy Kiple
Interior design: Beth McGill
Images: © Yolande de Kort / Trevillion Images

ISBN 978-0-8308-3191-3 (print)
ISBN 978-0-8308-9332-4 (digital)

Printed in the United States of America ∞

Library of Congress Cataloging-in-Publication Data
Names: Stott, John R. W., author. | Larsen, Dale, author. | Larsen, Sandy,
  author. | Stott, John R. W. Message of Romans.
Title: Reading Romans with John Stott / John Stott with Dale and Sandy Larsen
  ; with questions for groups or individuals.
Description: Downers Grove : InterVarsity Press, 2016. | Series: Reading the
  Bible with John Stott (RBJS) | "Vol. 1." | "This volume is abridged and
  edited from The Message of Romans..." | Includes bibliographical
  references.
Identifiers: LCCN 2016011664 (print) | LCCN 2016017713 (ebook) | ISBN
  9780830831913 (pbk. : alk. paper) | ISBN 9780830893324 (eBook)
Subjects: LCSH: Bible. Romans, I-VIII--Devotional literature.
Classification: LCC BS2665.54 .S76 2016 (print) | LCC BS2665.54 (ebook) | DDC
  227/.107--dc23
LC record available at https://lccn.loc.gov/2016011664

P	21	20	19	18	17	16	15	14	13	12	11	10	9	8	7	6	5	4	3	2	1
Y	34	33	32	31	30	29	28	27	26	25	24	23	22	21	20	19	18	17	16		

Contents

How to Read the Bible
with John Stott

During John Stott's life from 1921 to 2011, he was one of the world's master Bible teachers. Christians on every continent heard and read John Stott's exposition of Scripture, which was at once instructive and inspiring. With over eight million copies of his over fifty books sold in dozens of languages, it is not surprising that *Time* magazine recognized him in 2005 as one of the "100 Most Influential People in the World" and *Christianity Today* called him "evangelicalism's premier teacher and preacher." At the core of his ministry was the Bible and his beloved Bible Speaks Today series, which he originated as New Testament series editor. He himself contributed several volumes to the series, which have now been edited for this Reading the Bible with John Stott series.

The purpose of this volume is to offer excerpts of Stott's *The Message of Romans* in brief readings, suitable for daily use. Though Stott was himself an able scholar, this series avoids technicalities and scholarly debates, with each reading emphasizing the substance, significance and application of the text.

Following each set of six readings is a discussion guide. This can be used by individuals to help them dig more deeply into the text. It can also be used by study groups meeting regularly. Individuals in the groups can go through the six readings between group meetings and then use the discussion guide to help the group understand and apply the Scripture passage. Discussions are designed to last between forty-five and sixty minutes. Guidelines for leaders at the end of this volume offer many helpful suggestions for having a successful meeting.

If you are a group member, you can help everyone present in the following ways:

1. Read and pray through the readings before you meet.

2. Be willing to participate in the discussion. The leader won't be lecturing. Instead all will be asked to discuss what they have learned.

3. Stick to the topic being discussed and focus on the particular passage of Scripture. Only rarely should you refer to other portions of the Bible or outside sources. This will allow everyone to participate on equal footing.

4. Listen attentively to what others have to say. Be careful not to talk too much but encourage a balanced discussion among all participants. You may be surprised by what you can learn from others. Generally questions do not have one right answer but are intended to explore various dimensions of the text.

5. Expect God to teach you through the passage and through what others have to say.

6. Use the following guidelines and read them at the start of the first session:

- We will make the group a safe place by keeping confidential what is said in the group about personal matters.

- We will provide time for each person to talk who wants to.

- We will listen attentively to each other.

- We will talk about ourselves and our own situations, avoiding conversation about others.

- We will be cautious about giving advice to one another.

John Stott had an immense impact on the church in the last half of the twentieth century. With these volumes readers today can continue to benefit from the riches of the Bible that Stott opened to millions.

Introduction

❦

Ever since I became a Christian, I have enjoyed a love-hate relationship with Romans because of its joyful-painful personal challenges. It began soon after my conversion, with my longing to experience that death to sin which Romans 6 seemed to promise. I toyed for many years with the fantasy that Christians are supposed to be as insensitive to sin as a corpse is to external stimuli. My final deliverance from this illusion was sealed when I gave a series of talks on Romans 5–8. Next, Paul's devastating exposure of universal human sin and guilt in Romans 1:18–3:20 rescued me from that superficial evangelism which is preoccupied only with people's "felt needs." Then there was Romans 12 and its demand for our wholehearted commitment in response to God's mercies, and Romans 13, whose teaching about the use of force in the administration of justice made it impossible for me to remain a total pacifist. As for Romans 8, although I have declaimed its final triumphant verses at innumerable funerals, I have never lost the thrill of them.

Paul, although a man of his age who addressed his contemporaries, also speaks to all people of every age. I have not been surprised to observe how many contemporary issues Paul touches on in Romans: enthusiasm for evangelism in general and the propriety of Jewish evangelism in particular; whether homosexual relationships are natural or unnatural; whether we can still believe in such unfashionable concepts as God's wrath and propitiation; the historicity of Adam's fall and the origin of human death; the fundamental means to living a holy life; the place of law and of the Spirit in Christian discipleship; the distinction between assurance and presumption; the relation between divine sovereignty and human responsibility in salvation; the tension between ethnic identity and the solidarity of the body of Christ; relations between church and state; the respective duties of the individual citizen and the body politic; and how to handle differences of opinion within the Christian community. And this list is only a sample of the modern questions which, directly or indirectly, Romans raises and addresses.

Paul probably wrote the letter to the Romans from Corinth during the three months he spent in Greece (Acts 20:2). He mentions three places which he intends to visit: Jerusalem, Rome and Spain. Paul thought of Rome, being situated between Jerusalem and Spain, as a place of refreshment after he had been to Jerusalem and a place of preparation en route for Spain. His visits to Jerusalem and Spain were of special significance to him because they expressed his two continuing commitments: to the welfare of Israel (Jerusalem) and to the Gentile mission (Spain).

We still have to ask why Paul should write to the church in Rome. It was partly to prepare them for his visit. More than that, because he had not visited Rome before, and because most of the church members there were not known to him, he saw the need to establish his apostolic credentials by giving a full account of his gospel. With regard to his own situation, he sent them a threefold request—to pray that his service in Jerusalem would be acceptable, to help him on his way to Spain and to receive him during his stopover in Rome as the apostle to the Gentiles.

Paul's purposes in writing to the Romans are traceable not only to his own situation, however. His letter also arose from the situation in which the Roman Christians found themselves.

The church in Rome was a mixed community consisting of both Jews and Gentiles, with Gentiles in the majority, and there was considerable conflict between these groups. This conflict was primarily not ethnic (different races and cultures) but theological (different convictions about the status of God's covenant and law, and so about salvation). This controversy may be heard rumbling through Romans. And Paul is seen from beginning to end as an authentic peacemaker, anxious to preserve both truth and peace without sacrificing either to the other. As a patriotic Jew who had been specially commissioned as apostle to the Gentiles, he was in a unique position to be an agent of reconciliation. He was determined to make a full and fresh statement of the apostolic gospel, which would not compromise any of its revealed truths, but which would at the same time resolve the conflict between Jews and Gentiles over the covenant and the law, and so promote the unity of the church.

In his ministry of reconciliation, Paul develops two paramount themes and interweaves them beautifully. The first is the justification of guilty sinners by God's grace alone in Christ alone through faith alone, irrespective of either status or works. This is the most humbling and leveling of all Christian truths and experiences, and so is the fundamental basis of Christian unity. Paul's second theme is the consequent redefinition of the people of God, no longer according to descent, circumcision or culture, but according to faith in Jesus, so that all believers are the true children of Abraham, regardless of their ethnic origin or religious practice.

In writing on Romans, my first responsibility has been to seek a fresh encounter with the authentic Paul. My aim is to allow the apostle to say what he does say and not force him to say what we might want him to say.

At the beginning of his fourth-century exposition of Romans, Chrysostom spoke of how much he enjoyed hearing Paul's "spiritual trumpet." My prayer is that we may hear it again in our day and may readily respond to its summons.

John Stott

Romans 1:1-17
Gospel Power

🌿

Servant and Apostle

ROMANS 1:1-4

> ¹Paul, a servant of Christ Jesus, called to be an apostle and set apart for the gospel of God—²the gospel he promised beforehand through his prophets in the Holy Scriptures ³regarding his Son, who as to his earthly life was a descendant of David, ⁴and who through the Spirit of holiness was appointed the Son of God in power by his resurrection from the dead: Jesus Christ our Lord.

Paul begins his letter in a very personal way. He is evidently anxious from the start to establish a close relationship with his readers. He deviates from the letter-writing convention of his day by giving a much more elaborate description of himself than usual, in relation to the gospel. The probable reason is that he did not found the church in Rome. Nor has he yet visited it. He feels the need, therefore, to establish his credentials as an apostle and to summarize his gospel.

Paul identifies himself as "a servant of Jesus Christ, called to be an apostle and set apart for the gospel of God." Paul's twofold designation as *slave* (a better translation than *servant*) and *apostle* is particularly striking when these words are contrasted with one another. First, *slave* is a title of great humility; it expressed Paul's sense of personal insignificance, without rights of his own, having been purchased to belong to Christ. *Apostle*, on the other hand, was a title of great authority; it expressed his sense of official privilege and dignity by reason of his appointment by Jesus Christ. Second, *slave* is a general Christian word (every disciple looks to Jesus Christ as Lord), whereas *apostle* is a special title reserved for the Twelve and Paul and perhaps one or two others such as James.

Paul now proceeds to give an analysis of the gospel, for which he has been set apart.

The origin of the gospel is God. The apostles did not invent it; it was revealed and entrusted to them by God. This conviction underlies all authentic evangelism. What we have to share with others is neither a miscellany of human speculations, nor one more religion to add to the rest, nor really a religion at all. It is rather "the gospel of God," God's own good news for a lost world.

The Old Testament looks forward to the gospel. Although God revealed the gospel to the apostles, it did not come to them as a complete novelty, because he had already promised it through his prophets in Old Testament Scripture. There is an essential continuity between the Old Testament and the New. Both bear witness to Jesus Christ.

The substance of the gospel is Jesus Christ. Paul makes references, direct or indirect, to the birth (descended from David), death (presupposed by his resurrection), resurrection from the dead, and reign (on David's throne) of Jesus Christ. Here is a balanced statement of both the humiliation and the exaltation, the weakness and the power of God's Son, his human descent traced to David, his divine sonship-in-power established by the resurrection and gift of the Spirit.

This is the Christ, weak and powerful, incarnate and exalted, who owns and rules our lives.

Grace and Peace

ROMANS 1:5-7

5Through him we received grace and apostleship to call all the Gentiles to the obedience that comes from faith for his name's sake. 6And you also are among those Gentiles who are called to belong to Jesus Christ.

7To all in Rome who are loved by God and called to be his holy people:

Grace and peace to you from God our Father and from the Lord Jesus Christ.

As Paul goes on to state the purpose of his apostleship, he discloses further aspects of the gospel.

The scope of the gospel is all the nations. Paul defines its scope as "all the Gentiles." This seems to imply that the Christians in Rome were predominantly Gentile. Paul affirms that the gospel is for everybody; its scope is universal. Paul himself was a patriotic Jew who retained his love for his people and longed passionately for their salvation. At the same time, he had been called to be the apostle to the Gentiles. If we are to be committed to world mission, we too will have to be liberated from all pride of race, nation, tribe, caste and class, and acknowledge that God's gospel is for everybody, without exception and without distinction. This is a major theme of Romans.

The purpose of the gospel is the obedience of faith. In Romans, Paul insists more strongly than anywhere else that justification is through faith alone. Yet here he apparently writes that it is not by faith alone, but by obedience. Does the apostle contradict himself? No, we must give him credit for consistency of thought. This is the obedience that comes from faith, not the obedience of law. The proper response to the gospel is faith, indeed faith alone. Yet a true and living faith in Jesus Christ includes an element of submission (especially because its object is "Jesus Christ our Lord" [v. 4] or "the Lord Jesus Christ" [v. 7]) and leads inevitably into a lifetime of obedience.

Why did Paul desire to bring the nations to the obedience of faith? It was for the sake of the glory and honor of Christ's name. The highest of all missionary motives is neither obedience to the Great Commission (important as that is) nor love for sinners who are alienated and perishing (strong as that incentive is, especially when we contemplate the wrath of God), but burning and passionate zeal for the glory of Jesus Christ. Before this supreme goal of the Christian mission, all unworthy motives wither and die.

Thankful for Their Faith

ROMANS 1:8-13

⁸First, I thank my God through Jesus Christ for all of you, because your faith is being reported all over the world. ⁹God, whom I serve in my spirit in preaching the gospel of his Son, is my witness how constantly I remember you ¹⁰in my prayers at all times; and I pray that now at last by God's will the way may be opened for me to come to you.

¹¹I long to see you so that I may impart to you some spiritual gift to make you strong—¹²that is, that you and I may be mutually encouraged by each other's faith. ¹³I do not want you to be unaware, brothers and sisters, that I planned many times to come to you (but have been prevented from doing so until now) in order that I might have a harvest among you, just as I have had among the other Gentiles.

The apostle now tells his Roman readers frankly of his feelings toward them.

He thanks God for them all. The faith of the Romans is being reported all over the world. Wherever the church had spread, the news that there were Christians in the capital had spread also. Although Paul was not responsible for bringing the gospel to them, this does not inhibit him from giving thanks that Rome has been evangelized.

He prays for them. In Paul's apostolic ministry, preaching and praying go together. He assures them that, even though most of them are unknown to him personally, he intercedes for them *constantly* and *at all times*. In particular, he prays that "now at last by God's will," that is, if it is God's will, "the way may be opened" for him to come to them. Paul presumes neither to impose his will on God nor to claim to know what God's will may be. Instead, he submits his will to God's.

Paul longs to see the Christians in Rome, and he tells them why. He wants to impart to them some spiritual gift. He can hardly claim to be able to impart any spiritual gift himself. He appears to use the term in a more general sense. Perhaps he refers to his own teaching or exhortation, which he hopes to give them when he arrives. The statement seems indefinite, perhaps because he does not yet know what the Romans' main spiritual needs will be.

No sooner has Paul dictated these words than he seems to sense their inappropriate one-sidedness, as if he has everything to give and nothing to receive. So he immediately explains (even corrects) himself: "that is, that you and I may be mutually encouraged by each other's faith." He knows about the reciprocal blessings of Christian fellowship, and although he is an apostle, he is not too proud to acknowledge his need of it. Happy is the missionary who goes to another country and culture in the same spirit of receptivity, anxious to receive as well as give, to learn as well as teach, to be encouraged as well as to encourage! And happy is the congregation who have a pastor of the same humble mind!

So far Paul has been prevented from visiting Rome. Exactly what has foiled him he does not say. Perhaps his evangelistic work in and around Greece had not yet been completed. Why had he tried to visit them? He now gives a third reason: "in order that I might have [RSV "reap"] a harvest among you." Paul hopes to win some converts in Rome. It would be appropriate that the apostle to the Gentiles should engage in evangelistic reaping in the capital city of the Gentile world.

Gospel Debt

ROMANS 1:14-15

> [14]I am obligated both to Greeks and non-Greeks, both to the wise and the foolish. [15]That is why I am so eager to preach the gospel also to you who are in Rome.

Paul's words "I am obligated" should properly be translated "I am a debtor." There are two possible ways of getting into debt. The first is to borrow money *from* someone; the second is to be given money *for* someone by a third party. If a friend of yours had given me money to give to you, I would be in your debt until I handed it over. Your friend had put me in your debt.

It is in this second sense that Paul is in debt. He has not borrowed anything from the Romans which he must repay. Rather, Jesus Christ has entrusted him with the gospel for them. It is Jesus Christ who has made Paul a debtor by committing the gospel to his trust.

Paul was in debt to the Romans. As apostle to the Gentiles he was particularly in debt to the Gentile world. It was because of his sense of debt to them that he could write: "That is why I am so eager to preach the gospel also to you who are at Rome."

Similarly, we are debtors to the world, even though we are not apostles. Because the gospel has come to us, we have no liberty to keep it to ourselves. Nobody may claim a monopoly of the gospel. Good news is for sharing. We are under obligation to make it known to others. It is universally regarded as a dishonorable thing to leave a debt unpaid. We should be as eager to discharge our debt as Paul was to discharge his.

The Saving Power of God

ROMANS 1:16

> [16]For I am not ashamed of the gospel, because it is the power of God that brings salvation to everyone who believes: first to the Jew, then to the Gentile.

Some people are so offended by the thought that Paul could feel ashamed of the gospel that they pronounce his statement a sort of understatement for effect. But Jesus himself warned his disciples against being ashamed of him, which shows that he anticipated they might be (Mark 8:38). Paul gave Timothy a similar admonition (2 Timothy 1:8, 12). Paul knew that the message of the cross undermines self-righteousness and challenges self-indulgence. Whenever the gospel is faithfully preached, it arouses opposition, often contempt and sometimes ridicule.

How then did Paul (and how shall we) overcome the temptation to be ashamed of the gospel? By remembering that the same message which some people despise for its weakness is in fact "the power of God that brings salvation to everyone who believes." We know this because we have experienced its saving power in our own lives. God has reconciled us to himself through Christ, forgiven our sins, made us his children, put his Spirit within us, begun to transform us and introduced us into his new community. How can we possibly be ashamed of the gospel?

Moreover, the gospel brings salvation to "everyone who believes: first to the Jew, then to the Gentile." Saving faith is the great leveler. Everyone who is saved is saved in exactly the same way, by faith. That goes for Jews and Gentiles equally. There is no distinction between them.

Paul's eagerness to evangelize in Rome arose from his recognition that the gospel is an unpaid debt to the world and the saving power of God. The first gave him a sense of obligation (he had been entrusted with the good news), and the second gave him a sense of conviction (if it had saved him, it could save others). Still today the gospel is both a debt to discharge and a power to experience.

God's Righteousness Revealed

ROMANS 1:17

> ¹⁷For in the gospel the righteousness of God is revealed—
> a righteousness that is by faith from first to last, just as it
> is written: "The righteous will live by faith."

The reason the gospel is God's saving power is that in it God's righteousness is revealed. Moreover, this righteousness is "by faith from first to last," in fulfillment of Habakkuk 2:4: "the righteous person will live by his faithfulness."

Throughout Romans, Paul is at pains to defend the righteous character and behavior of God. For he is convinced that whatever God does in salvation or in judgment is absolutely consistent with his righteousness. And in Romans, God's personal righteousness is supremely seen in the cross of Christ.

The righteousness of God revealed in the gospel is the righteous status which God requires if we are ever to stand before him, which he achieves through the atoning sacrifice of the cross, which he reveals in the gospel, and which he bestows freely on all who trust in Jesus Christ. It is God's righteous initiative in putting sinners right with himself, by bestowing on them a righteousness not their own but his. The righteousness of God is God's just justification of the unjust, his righteous way of pronouncing the unrighteous righteous, in which he both demonstrates his righteousness and gives righteousness to us. He has done it through Christ, the righteous one, who died for the unrighteous, as Paul will explain later. And he does it by faith when we put our trust in him and cry to him for mercy.

This righteousness of God, which is revealed in the gospel and offered to us, is literally "out of faith into faith" *or* "from faith to faith." Many scholars, however, translate Paul's quotation of Habakkuk differently: "he who through faith is righteous shall live." Is it legitimate to translate the Habakkuk text in this way, and so to make faith the way to righteousness instead of the way to life? I think so. Whichever way the sentence is understood, both renderings affirm that "the righteous will live" and that faith is essential. The only question is whether the righteous by faith will live, or the righteous will live by faith. Are not both true? Righteousness and life are both by faith. Those who are righteous by faith also live by faith. Having begun in faith, they continue in the same path.

Romans 1:1-17

....

Discussion Guide

OPEN
When and how did you first come in contact with the power of the gospel?

STUDY
Read Romans 1:1-17.

1. What information about the gospel do you find in this passage?

2. Paul says in that through the gospel we are "called to belong" (v. 6). How have you experienced that sense of belonging?

3. In verse 5 Paul speaks of "obedience that comes from faith." How are obedience and faith naturally connected?

4. Review verses 1-7. What do you learn about Paul? What do you learn about the Romans?

5. In what different ways does Paul express his affection for the Romans (vv. 8-15)?

6. What do these verses reveal about Paul's relationship with God?

7. Although Paul is an apostle, he is not too proud to acknowledge his need for the reciprocal blessings of Christian fellowship. In verse 12 he says that he hopes that he and the Romans will be "mutually encouraged by each other's faith." Why is mutual encouragement valuable to Christians?

8. Focus on Paul's declaration in verses 16-17. What do these verses reveal about the power of the gospel?

9. This passage uses important words like *gospel, salvation, righteousness* and *faith*. How are these terms related to each other?

10. This section of Paul's letter ends with the famous phrase "The righteous will live by faith." In practical terms, what does this mean?

APPLY

1. What power have you seen the gospel exercise in your life?

2. What power would you like it to have?

3. Paul says in verses 15-16, "I am so eager to preach. . . . I am not ashamed of the gospel." What can you do that expresses a similar enthusiasm for Christ?

Romans 1:18-32
A Downward Spiral

❧

The Wrath of God

ROMANS 1:18-19

> ¹⁸The wrath of God is being revealed from heaven against all the godlessness and wickedness of people, who suppress the truth by their wickedness, ¹⁹since what may be known about God is plain to them, because God has made it plain to them.

The very mention of God's wrath these days is likely to cause people embarrassment and even incredulity. How can anger, they ask, which Jesus in the Sermon on the Mount equated with murder (Matthew 5:22) and which Paul identified as a manifestation of our sinful human nature (Galatians 5:19-20), possibly be attributed to the all-holy God?

The wrath of God is almost totally different from human anger. It does not mean that God loses his temper, flies into a rage or is ever malicious, spiteful or vindictive. His wrath is his holy hostility to evil, his refusal to condone it or come to terms with it, his just judgment upon it.

In general, the wrath of God is directed against evil alone. We get angry when our pride has been wounded, but there is no personal pique in the anger of God. Nothing arouses it except evil, and evil always does. God's wrath is directed not against godlessness and wickedness in a vacuum, but against the godlessness and wickedness of those people "who suppress the truth by their wickedness." They have decided to live for themselves rather than for God and others, and therefore they deliberately stifle any truth that challenges their self-centeredness.

God's wrath will be revealed in the future judgment of the last day, and there is a present disclosure of it in the public administration of justice. However, there is another kind of present disclosure of the anger of God, "being revealed from heaven." God abandons stubborn sinners to their willful self-centeredness, and the resulting process of moral and spiritual degeneration is to be understood as a judicial act of God.

In summary, God's wrath is his settled and perfectly righteous antagonism to evil. It is directed against people who have some knowledge of God's truth through the created order but deliberately suppress it in order to pursue their own self-centered path. And it is already being revealed in the moral and social corruption that Paul saw in much of the Greco-Roman world of his day and that we can see in the permissive societies of our day.

Revelation Through Creation

ROMANS 1:20

> [20]For since the creation of the world God's invisible qualities—his eternal power and divine nature—have been clearly seen, being understood from what has been made, so that people are without excuse.

The God who is invisible and unknowable has made himself both visible and knowable through what he has made. The creation is a visible disclosure of the invisible God, an intelligible disclosure of the otherwise unknown God. Just as artists reveal themselves in what they draw, paint and sculpt, so the divine Artist has revealed himself in his creation.

The truth of revelation through creation is a regular theme of Scripture. "The heavens declare the glory of God" (Psalm 19:1) and "the whole earth is full of his glory" (Isaiah 6:3).

God's self-revelation through "what has been made" has four main characteristics. It is *general* because it is made to everybody everywhere, as opposed to *special* because it is only to particular people in particular places, through Christ and the biblical authors. It is *natural* because it comes through the natural order, as opposed to *supernatural*, involving the incarnation of the Son and the inspiration of the Scriptures. It is *continuous* because since the creation of the world it has gone on "day after day . . . night after night" (Psalm 19:2) as opposed to *final* and finished in Christ and in Scripture. And it is *creational*, revealing God's glory through creation, as opposed to *salvific*, revealing God's grace in Christ.

The conviction that God reveals himself through the created universe is still meaningful to us today. Through general revelation people can know God's power, deity and glory, although not his saving grace through Christ. This knowledge is enough not to save them but rather to condemn them, because they do not live up to it. Instead, they *suppress the truth by their wickedness*, so that they *are without excuse*. It is against this willful human rebellion that God's wrath is revealed.

Nobody can plead innocence because nobody can plead ignorance. Anthropologists have also found a worldwide moral sense in human beings so that, although conscience is of course to some extent conditioned by culture, it still testifies to everybody everywhere both that there is a difference between right and wrong, and that evil deserves to be punished.

A Foolish Exchange

ROMANS 1:21-25

21For although they knew God, they neither glorified him as God nor gave thanks to him, but their thinking became futile and their foolish hearts were darkened. 22Although they claimed to be wise, they became fools 23and exchanged the glory of the immortal God for images made to look like a mortal human being and birds and animals and reptiles.

24Therefore God gave them over in the sinful desires of their hearts to sexual impurity for the degrading of their bodies with one another. 25They exchanged the truth about

God for a lie, and worshiped and served created things
rather than the Creator—who is forever praised. Amen.

Paul's statement that the suppressers of truth "knew God" cannot
be taken absolutely, since elsewhere Paul writes that people outside
Christ do not know God. Rather it refers to the limited knowledge
of God's power and glory which is available to everybody through
general revelation.

Instead of their knowledge of God leading to the worship of
God, people chose not to glorify or honor him. Despite their
claim to wisdom, they became fools. Their futility, darkness and
folly were seen in their idolatry and in the absurd exchange that
their idolatry involved: to "exchange the glory of the immortal
God" for images of mortal creatures. While the worship of
images is obviously foolish, the modern obsession with wealth,
fame and power is equally foolish and equally blameworthy.

God's judgment on the people's idolatry was to give them
over "in the sinful desires of their hearts to sexual impurity." The
history of the world confirms that idolatry tends to immorality.
A false image of God leads to a false understanding of sex. Paul
does not tell us what kind of immorality he has in mind, except
that it involved "the degrading of their bodies with one another."
Illicit sex degrades people's humanness; sex in marriage, as God
intended, ennobles humanness.

Paul goes on to mention another exchange: exchanging "the
truth of God for a lie." The falsehood of idolatry is the ultimate
lie. It involves transferring our worship to "created things" from
the "Creator," whom Paul in a spontaneous doxology declares
worthy of eternal adoration: "who is forever praised."

Shameful Lusts

ROMANS 1:26-27

> [26]Because of this, God gave them over to shameful lusts.
> Even their women exchanged natural sexual relations for
> unnatural ones. [27]In the same way the men also aban-
> doned natural relations with women and were inflamed
> with lust for one another. Men committed shameful acts
> with other men, and received in themselves the due
> penalty for their error.

Paul's words are a crucial text in the debate about homosexuality.
He writes that God gave people over to "shameful lusts,"
which he specifies as lesbian homosexual practices. In both
cases the people concerned are guilty of exchanging natural
relations for unnatural.

The traditional interpretation of Paul's words, that they
describe and condemn all homosexual behavior, is being chal-
lenged. Some homosexual people are urging that their relationships cannot be described as unnatural, since they are
perfectly natural to them. We have no liberty to interpret the
noun *nature* to meaning *my* nature, or the adjective *natural*
to mean *what seems natural to me*. To act against nature means
to violate the order that God has established, while to act
according to nature means to behave in line with what the
Creator intended.

Genesis tells us the Creator's intent, and Jesus confirmed
it: "at the beginning the Creator 'made them male and female,'
and said, 'For this reason a man will leave his father and

mother and be united to his wife, and the two will become one flesh.' So they are no longer two, but one flesh." Jesus added his personal endorsement and deduction: "Therefore what God has joined together, let no one separate" (Matthew 19:4-6, quoting Genesis 2:24). God created humankind male and female; God instituted marriage as a heterosexual union; and what God has united, we have no liberty to separate. This threefold action of God established that the only context which he intends for the "one flesh" experience is heterosexual monogamy, and that a homosexual partnership (however loving and committed it may claim to be) is against nature and can never be regarded as a legitimate alternative to marriage.

Filled with Wickedness

ROMANS 1:28-31

> [28]Furthermore, just as they did not think it worthwhile to retain the knowledge of God, so God gave them over to a depraved mind, so that they do what ought not to be done. [29]They have become filled with every kind of wickedness, evil, greed and depravity. They are full of envy, murder, strife, deceit and malice. They are gossips, [30]slanderers, God-haters, insolent, arrogant and boastful; they invent ways of doing evil; they disobey their parents; [31]they have no understanding, no fidelity, no love, no mercy.

Paul's statement in verse 28 about idolaters includes a play on words in the Greek something like "Since they did not see fit to retain the knowledge of God, he gave them over to an unfit mind." The depraved mind of the idolaters led to a whole variety of antisocial practices, which Paul says "ought not to be done." Taken together, these acts describe the breakdown of human community, as standards disappear and society disintegrates. Paul gives a catalog of twenty-one vices. Such lists were not uncommon in those days in Stoic, Jewish and early Christian literature.

The list of sins defies neat classification. It begins with four general sins that these people have become filled with, namely, "every kind of wickedness, evil, greed and depravity." Then come five more sins that all depict broken human relationships: "envy, murder, strife, deceit and malice." Next come a couple of sins standing on their own, which seem to refer to libel and slander. These two are followed by four that seem to portray different and extreme forms of pride: "God-haters, insolent, arrogant and boastful."

Now comes another pair of words, denoting people who are inventive in relation to evil and rebellious in relation to parents. The list ends with four negatives: "foolish, faithless, heartless, ruthless" (RSV).

Paul presents a dismal list of ways in which humanity rebels against God. Yet even as he demonstrates the universality of human sin, he never loses sight of the good news of Christ. Paul heads this section in Romans 1:17 with "The righteousness of God" (his righteous way of "righteousing" the unrighteous), which is the only possible context in which Paul could dare to expose the squalor of human unrighteousness.

A Summary of Sin

ROMANS 1:32

> ³²Although they know God's righteous decree that those who do such things deserve death, they not only continue to do these very things but also approve of those who practice them.

The last verse of Romans 1 is a concluding summary of the human perversity Paul has been describing. First, "they know." Again he begins with the knowledge possessed by the people he is depicting. It is not now God's truth that they know, however, but "God's righteous decree," namely, "that those who do such things deserve death." As Paul will write later, "the wages of sin is death" (Romans 6:23). And they know it. Their conscience condemns them.

Nevertheless, they disregard their knowledge. "They not only continue to do these very things," which they know deserve death, *but* (which is worse) they actively encourage others to do the same and so flagrantly "approve" the evil behavior that God has expressed his disapproval of.

We have come to the end of Paul's portrayal of depraved Gentile society. Its essence lies in the antithesis between what people know and what they do. God's wrath is specifically directed against those who deliberately suppress truth for the sake of evil.

Nothing keeps people away from Christ more than their inability to see their need of him or their unwillingness to admit it. As Jesus put it, "It is not the healthy who need a doctor, but the sick. I have not come to call the righteous, but sinners" (Mark 2:17). He did not mean that some people, like the doctor, *are* righteous, so that they do not need salvation, but that some people *think* they are. In that condition of self-righteousness they will never come to Christ. For just as we go to the doctor only when we admit that we are ill and cannot cure ourselves, so we will go to Christ only when we admit that we are guilty sinners and cannot save ourselves.

The same principle applies to all our difficulties. Deny the problem, and nothing can be done about it; admit the problem, and at once there is the possibility of a solution. To be sure, some people protest boldly that they are neither sinful nor guilty, and that they do not need Christ. It would be wrong to seek to induce guilty feelings in people artificially. But because sin and guilt are universal, we cannot leave people alone in their false paradise of supposed innocence. It is this plain and unpopular principle which lies behind Paul's writing in the first part of Romans.

Romans 1:18-32

....

DISCUSSION GUIDE

OPEN

What comes to your mind when you think of "the wrath of God"?

STUDY

Read Romans 1:18-32.

1. Verse 18 begins "The wrath of God is being revealed." Why does that happen according to verses 18-23?

2. Paul says these people are "without excuse" (v. 20). What, according to verses 18-20, is the reason for that?

3. Mentally review some of your own experiences with God's creation. What do these reveal to you about God?

4. What is dangerous about knowing about God but not acting on that knowledge (vv. 21-23)?

5. What do you think would happen to a person whose heart is "darkened" as verse 21 describes?

6. Three times in verses 24-32, Paul repeats the phrase "God gave them over." What did God give them over to?

7. What is your mental picture of each of these three downward spirals?

8. Paul lists sins like envy and murder, arrogance and God-hating, faithlessness and ruthlessness in verses 29-30. What does the variety in this list suggest about the nature of sin?

9. What makes you uneasy about verses 18-32?

10. In verses 24, 26 and 28, God gave the people what they wanted. Why are these kinds of temptations dangerous?

11. Paul concludes in verse 32 that these people deserve spiritual death. Why?

APPLY

1. What sins in this downward spiral do you personally need to work on resisting?

2. What do you know about God that would help keep you out of this downward spiral?

3

Romans 2:1–3:8

God's Fairness

❦

Inescapable Judgment

ROMANS 2:1-4

> ¹You, therefore, have no excuse, you who pass judgment on someone else, for at whatever point you judge another, you are condemning yourself, because you who pass judgment do the same things. ²Now we know that God's judgment against those who do such things is based on truth. ³So when you, a mere human being, pass judgment on them and yet do the same things, do you think you will escape God's judgment? ⁴Or do you show contempt for the riches of his kindness, forbearance and patience, not realizing that God's kindness is intended to lead you to repentance?

Having declared the depraved Gentile world to be guilty and inexcusable, Paul now passes the same verdict on an imaginary character whom he addresses in direct speech: "You, therefore, have no excuse, you who pass judgment on someone else."

Paul's main emphasis is clearly seen in his turning from the world of shameless immorality (Romans 1:18-32) to the world of self-conscious moralism. He seems to be confronting every human being (Jew or Gentile) who is a moralizer, who presumes to pass moral judgments on other people.

Paul uncovers a strange human foible, our tendency to be critical of everybody except ourselves. We are often as harsh in our judgment of others as we are lenient toward ourselves. We work ourselves into a state of self-righteous indignation over the disgraceful behavior of other people, while the same behavior seems not nearly so serious when it is ours. We even gain a vicarious satisfaction from condemning in others the same faults we excuse in ourselves. In doing so, we expose ourselves to the judgment of God, and we leave ourselves without either excuse or escape. For if our critical faculties are so well developed that we become experts in our moral evaluation of others, we can hardly plead ignorance of moral issues ourselves.

Paul does not ask us either to suspend our critical faculties or to renounce all criticism and rebuke of others. Rather he means to prohibit our standing in judgment on other people and condemning them, especially when we fail to condemn ourselves. For this is the hypocrisy of the double standard, a high standard for other people and a comfortably low one for ourselves.

Sometimes, in a futile attempt to escape "God's judgment," we take refuge in a theological argument. We appeal to God's character, especially to "the riches of his kindness, forbearance and patience." We maintain that he is much too kind and longsuffering to punish anybody, and therefore we can sin with impunity. But this kind of manipulative theologizing shows contempt rather than honor for God. It is not faith; it is presumption. God's kindness leads us toward repentance. It is intended to give us space in which to repent, not to give us an excuse for sinning.

Righteous Judgment

ROMANS 2:5-11

> [5]But because of your stubbornness and your unrepentant heart, you are storing up wrath against yourself for the day of God's wrath, when his righteous judgment will be revealed. [6]God "will repay each person according to what they have done." [7]To those who by persistence in doing good seek glory, honor and immortality, he will give eternal life. [8]But for those who are self-seeking and who reject the truth and follow evil, there will be wrath and anger. [9]There will be trouble and distress for every human being who does evil: first for the Jew, then for the Gentile; [10]but glory, honor and peace for everyone who does good: first for the Jew, then for the Gentile. [11]For God does not show favoritism.

Does Paul contradict himself? Does he begin by declaring that salvation is by faith alone, then destroy his own gospel by saying that it is by good works after all?

No, Paul is not contradicting himself. He affirms that, although justification is indeed by faith, judgment will be according to works. The day of judgment will be a public occasion. Its purpose will be less to determine God's judgment than to announce it and to vindicate it. The divine judgment, which is a process of sifting and separating, is going on secretly all the time, as people range themselves for or against Christ, but on the last day its results will be made public. Such a public occasion, on which a public verdict will be given and a public sentence passed, will require public and verifiable evidence to support them. And the only public evidence available will be our works, what we have done and have been seen to do. The presence or absence of saving faith in our hearts will be disclosed by the presence or absence of good works of love in our lives.

The two final destinies of humankind are called "eternal life," which Jesus defined in terms of knowing him and knowing the Father, and "wrath and anger," the awful outpouring of God's judgment. The basis of this separation will be a combination of what we seek (our ultimate goal in life) and what we do (our actions in the service either of ourselves or of others). It is very similar to the teaching of Jesus in the Sermon on the Mount, in which he delineated the alternative human ambitions of seeking our material welfare versus seeking God's kingdom, and the alternative human activities of practicing versus not practicing his teaching. Those who seek God and persevere in goodness will receive eternal life, while those who are self-seeking and follow evil will experience God's wrath.

Paul simplifies the two categories of people into "every human being who does evil" and "everyone who does good." Paul then elaborates the two destinies. One is "trouble and distress," emphasizing its anguish, and the other is "glory" and "honor" (verse 7) and adding "peace," that comprehensive word for reconciled relationships with God and with each other. In both cases Paul adds "first for the Jew, then for the Gentile," affirming the priority of the Jew in judgment and in salvation, and thus declaring the absolute impartiality of God.

Impartial Judgment

ROMANS 2:12-16

> [12]All who sin apart from the law will also perish apart from the law, and all who sin under the law will be judged by the law. [13]For it is not those who hear the law who are righteous in God's sight, but it is those who obey the law who will be declared righteous. [14](Indeed, when Gentiles, who do not have the law, do by nature things required by the law, they are a law for themselves, even though they do not have the law. [15]They show that the requirements of the law are written on their hearts, their consciences also bearing witness, and their thoughts sometimes accusing them and at other times even defending them.) [16]This will take place on the day when God judges people's secrets through Jesus Christ, as my gospel declares.

God does not show favoritism. God's judgment is impartial, whether of Jews or of Gentiles. These two groups appear to be quite different because Jews "hear the law," while Gentiles "do not have the law." Yet, Paul insists, this difference can be exaggerated since "the requirements of the law are written on" all human "hearts." Jews and Gentiles are both subject to sin and death.

All who have sinned "apart from the law [Gentiles] will also perish apart from the law." They will not be judged by a standard they have not known. They will perish because of their sin, not because of their ignorance of the law. God created them as self-conscious moral persons. Although they do not have the law in their hands, they do have its requirements in their hearts because God has written them there.

Similarly, all who have sinned "under the law [Jews] will be judged by the law." They too will be judged by the standard they have known. God will be absolutely evenhanded in judgment.

The universal knowledge of God's law is an indispensable basis of divine judgment. God has no favorites, Jews and Gentiles will be judged by him without discrimination, and both groups have some knowledge of God's law. Consequently, no human being can plead complete ignorance. We have all sinned against a moral law we have known. Whether we have come to know it by special or general revelation, by grace or nature, outwardly or inwardly, in the Scripture or in the heart, is largely irrelevant. The point is that all human beings have known something of God and of goodness, but have suppressed the truth in order to indulge in wickedness. So we all come under the righteous judgment of God.

God's law is also a basis of Christian mission, whether evangelism or social action. Some say we should not try to induce feelings of guilt that people do not have. This is a misconception. We are moral beings by creation. That is to say, not only do we experience an inner urge to do what we believe to be right, but we also have a sense of guilt and remorse when we have done what we know to be wrong. This is an essential feature of our humanness. There is of course such a thing as false guilt. But guilt feelings that are aroused by wrongdoing are healthy. These feelings rebuke us for betraying our humanity, and they impel us to seek forgiveness in Christ. In all evangelism, I find it a constant encouragement to say to myself, "The other person's conscience is on my side."

Securing justice in society is a further implication of Paul's teaching. Every human community has a basic recognition of the difference between right and wrong, an accepted set of values. This has important social and political implications. It means that legislators and educators can assume that God's law is good for society and that at least to some degree people know it. It is not a case of Christians trying to force their standards on an unwilling public, but of helping the public to see that God's law is "for our own good at all times," because it is the law of human beings and of human community. If democracy is government by consent, consent depends on consensus, consensus on argument, and argument on ethical apologists who will develop a case for the goodness of God's law.

Misplaced Confidence

ROMANS 2:17-24

[17]Now you, if you call yourself a Jew; if you rely on the law and boast in God; [18]if you know his will and approve of what is superior because you are instructed by the law; [19]if you are convinced that you are a guide for the blind, a light for those who are in the dark, [20]an instructor of the foolish, a teacher of little children,

because you have in the law the embodiment of knowledge and truth—[21]you, then, who teach others, do you not teach yourself? You who preach against stealing, do you steal? [22]You who say that people should not commit adultery, do you commit adultery? You who abhor idols, do you rob temples? [23]You who boast in the law, do you dishonor God by breaking the law? [24]As it is written: "God's name is blasphemed among the Gentiles because of you."

In his wide-ranging critique of the human race, Paul now moves on from critical moralizers in general, whether Jews or Gentiles, to Jewish people in particular in their self-confidence. Here he gives a straightforward account of Jewish people in their double relation to the law. Being instructed, they instruct. Being taught, they teach.

But now Paul turns the tables on them. They do not live up to their knowledge. They do not practice what they preach. So he asks five rhetorical questions, which draw attention to their inconsistency.

The first is general: "You, then, who teach others, do you not teach yourself?" It is followed by three questions about particular sins: "You who preach against stealing, do you steal? You who say that people should not commit adultery, do you commit adultery? You who abhor idols, do you rob temples?" Although Jews would have recoiled from the implications of idolatry, adultery and theft, Paul wants us to think of Jesus' teaching in the Sermon on the Mount about the thoughts of our hearts.

Paul's fifth rhetorical question is again more general: "You who boast in the law [which the Jews did, see verse 17], do you dishonor God by breaking the law? As it is written, 'God's name is blasphemed among the Gentiles because of you.'" This quotation seems to combine Isaiah 52:5 and Ezekiel 36:22. In both texts God's name had been mocked because his people had been defeated and enslaved. Could the Lord not protect his own people? Just so, moral defeat, like military defeat, brings discredit on the name of God.

The argument of this passage is just as applicable to us as to first-century critical moralizers and self-confident Jews. If we judge others, we should be able to judge ourselves. If we teach others, we should be able to teach ourselves. If we set ourselves up as either teachers or judges of others, we can have no excuse if we do not teach or judge ourselves. We cannot possibly plead ignorance of moral rectitude. On the contrary, we invite God's condemnation of our hypocrisy.

The Real Jew

ROMANS 2:25-29

> [25]Circumcision has value if you observe the law, but if you break the law, you have become as though you had not been circumcised. [26]So then, if those who are not circumcised keep the law's requirements, will they not be regarded as though they were circumcised? [27]The one who is not circumcised physically and yet obeys the law will condemn you who, even though you have the written code and circumcision, are a lawbreaker.

[28]A person is not a Jew who is one only outwardly, nor is circumcision merely outward and physical. [29]No, a person is a Jew who is one inwardly; and circumcision is circumcision of the heart, by the Spirit, not by the written code. Such a person's praise is not from other people, but from God.

Circumcision was a God-given sign and seal of God's covenant with the Jews. But it was not a magical ceremony or a charm. It did not provide them with permanent insurance against the wrath of God. It was no substitute for obedience; it constituted rather a commitment to obedience. Yet the Jews had an almost superstitious confidence in the saving power of their circumcision.

Paul counters this false assurance by pointing out that circumcision is the sign of covenant membership, and covenant membership demands obedience. The ultimate sign of membership of the covenant of God is neither circumcision nor possession of the law, but the obedience that both circumcision and the law demand. The Jews' circumcision did not make them what their disobedience proved they were not. This is not salvation by obedience but obedience as the evidence of salvation. The corollary is that Jews are just as much exposed to the judgment of God as Gentiles.

This extraordinary reversal of roles, by which the Gentile condemns the Jew instead of the Jew condemning the Gentile, is due to a necessary redefinition of Jewish identity. A person is a Jew who is one "inwardly." True circumcision is circumcision of the heart, by the Spirit. This concept is not new with

Paul, since it occurs regularly in the Old Testament. But Paul looks for something more: a circumcision of the heart which will *replace* the physical sign. It will be an inward work of the Holy Spirit, which the law as an external written code could never accomplish.

In his redefinition of what it means to be a Jew, an authentic member of God's covenant people, Paul draws a fourfold contrast. The essence of being a true Jew (who may be ethnically a Gentile) is not something outward and visible, but inward and invisible. True circumcision is in the heart, not the flesh. It is effected by the Spirit, not the law. It wins the approval of God rather than human beings.

Human beings are comfortable with what is outward, visible, material and superficial. But what matters to God is a deep, inward, secret work of the Holy Spirit in our hearts.

Some Objections Answered

ROMANS 3:1-8

¹What advantage, then, is there in being a Jew, or what value is there in circumcision? ²Much in every way! First of all, the Jews have been entrusted with the very words of God.

³What if some were unfaithful? Will their unfaithfulness nullify God's faithfulness? ⁴Not at all! Let God be true, and every human being a liar. As it is written:

"So that you may be proved right when you speak
    and prevail when you judge."

⁵But if our unrighteousness brings out God's righteousness more clearly, what shall we say? That God is
unjust in bringing his wrath on us? (I am using a human
argument.) ⁶Certainly not! If that were so, how could God
judge the world? ⁷Someone might argue, "If my falsehood
enhances God's truthfulness and so increases his glory,
why am I still condemned as a sinner?" ⁸Why not say—as
some slanderously claim that we say—"Let us do evil that
good may result"? Their condemnation is just!

It is not difficult to imagine the reactions of at least some of Paul's
Jewish readers: a mixture of incredulity and indignation. His thesis
will have seemed to them an outrageous undermining of the very
foundations of Judaism, namely, God's character and covenant.

Paul's method of handling Jewish objections to his teaching
takes the form of a dialogue, first posing questions, then answering
them. It is probable that he is reconstructing the actual arguments
Jews have flung at him during his synagogue evangelism.

The first objection is that Paul's teaching undermines God's
covenant. If the words *Jew* and *circumcision* are now to be radically redefined, then what advantage is there in being a Jew or in
circumcision? They have much value in every way, but a different
kind of value, that is, responsibility rather than security. To be the
custodians of God's special revelation was an immensely privileged responsibility; it had been given to no other nation.

The second objection is that Paul's teaching nullifies God's
faithfulness. If God's people are unfaithful, does that necessarily
mean that God is unfaithful? Paul's retort is more forceful than
is suggested by the expression "Certainly not!" For God will

never break his covenant. Even if every single human being were a liar, God would still be true, because he remains invariably himself and true to himself.

The third objection is that Paul's teaching calls God's justice into question. According to Paul's teaching, says the objector, our unrighteousness benefits God, because it displays his character all the more brightly. Would it not be unfair of God to punish people for something that is to his advantage? Paul asks a counterquestion: if God really were unjust, how could he judge the world? Paul takes it as axiomatic that God is the universal judge and that therefore, as Abraham said, the Judge of all the earth will do right.

The fourth objection is that Paul's teaching falsely promotes God's glory. Are we not doing God a service by sinning and therefore manifesting his glory by contrast? Paul was even falsely accused of promoting this perverse idea. But no good results can justify the encouragement of evil. Evil never promotes the glory of God.

Paul saw that the character of God was at stake. So he reaffirmed God's covenant as having abiding value, God's faithfulness to his promises, God's justice as judge, and God's true glory, which is promoted only by good, never by evil.

Romans 2:1–3:8

....

DISCUSSION GUIDE

OPEN

If you could live your life without personal guilt or judgment, would you choose to do so? Explain your response.

STUDY

Read Romans 2:1–3:8.

1. What is the difference between human judgment and God's judgment (2:1-4)?

2. Look more carefully at verse 4. How might God's judgment be a kindness?

3. Focus on verses 5-11. What does this passage reveal about the day of God's wrath?

4. According to these verses, what is the relationship between God's law and his judgment?

5. What example do you see of God's fairness when he judges Gentiles, who did not have his law as a part of their history?

6. Verse 15 speaks of the conscience. Why is a conscience important in this setting?

7. The people described in verses 17-29 assumed that they had a good relationship with God. What kinds of things did they depend on to give them that relationship?

8. What is Paul trying to show his readers with the list of questions in verses 21-23?

9. What is the relationship between circumcision and keeping the law (vv. 25-29)?

10. What does it mean to have a circumcised heart (v. 29)?

11. How have you sensed the Spirit at work in your heart?

12. In what ways had the Jews "been entrusted with the very words of God" (3:2)?

13. How would you respond to a person who said, "I'm glad I fell so deeply into wrong. It shows how good God is and how much he will forgive" (3:5-8)?

APPLY

1. Several times this passage speaks of the day of God's wrath. How would you advise someone to prepare for that day?

2. God (who is perfect) shows no favoritism in his judgments. What are some ways you can practice fairness in your own actions?

3. The Jews Paul was writing to had all sorts of misplaced confidence about their special relationship with God. What or whom have you been tempted to trust besides the grace of Jesus Christ alone?

4

Romans 3:9-26
Unholy Togetherness

❧

Jews and Gentiles Alike

ROMANS 3:9

> ⁹What shall we conclude then? Do we have any advantage?
> Not at all! For we have already made the charge that Jews
> and Gentiles alike are all under the power of sin.

Approaching the end of his lengthy argument, the apostle asks
himself how to wrap it all up, how to rest his case. He has exposed in succession the blatant unrighteousness of much of the
ancient Gentile world (Romans 1:18-32), the hypocritical righteousness of moralizers (Romans 2:1-16) and the confident self-
righteousness of Jewish people, whose anomaly is that they
boast of God's law but break it (Romans 2:17–3:8). So now Paul
arraigns and condemns the whole human race.

Paul asks the same question twice within the space of a few
verses and proceeds to give apparently opposite answers. In
Romans 3:1 he asked, "What advantage, then, is there in being

a Jew?" And he answered, "Much in every way!" Now he asks, "Do we [Jews] have any advantage?" And he replies, "Not at all!" He sounds as if he is contradicting himself, asserting first that there is great advantage in being a Jew and then that there is none.

How can we resolve this discrepancy? Only by clarifying what "advantage" Paul has in mind. If he means privilege and responsibility, then the Jews have much because God has entrusted his revelation to them. But if he means favoritism, then the Jews have none, because God will not exempt them from judgment. "We have already made the charge [in Romans 1:18–2:29] that Jews and Gentiles alike are all under the power of sin." Paul almost personifies sin as a cruel tyrant who holds the human race imprisoned in guilt and under judgment. Sin is on top of us, weighs us down, and is a crushing burden.

No One Is Righteous

ROMANS 3:10-18

> ¹⁰As it is written:
> "There is no one righteous, not even one;
>> ¹¹there is no one who understands;
>> there is no one who seeks God.
> ¹²All have turned away,
>> they have together become worthless;
>> there is no one who does good,
>> not even one."
> ¹³"Their throats are open graves;

their tongues practice deceit."

"The poison of vipers is on their lips."

[14]"Their mouths are full of cursing and bitterness."

[15]"Their feet are swift to shed blood;

[16]ruin and misery mark their ways,

[17]and the way of peace they do not know."

[18]"There is no fear of God before their eyes."

Paul supplies a series of seven Old Testament quotations, the first probably from Ecclesiastes, then five from the Psalms and one from Isaiah, all of which bear witness in different ways to human unrighteousness. Three features of this grim biblical picture stand out.

First, it declares the ungodliness of sin. In fact Scripture identifies the essence of sin as ungodliness. Sin is the revolt of the self against God, the dethronement of God with a view to the enthronement of oneself. Ultimately, sin is self-deification, the reckless determination to occupy the throne that belongs to God alone.

Second, this chain of Old Testament verses teaches the pervasiveness of sin. Sin affects every part of our human constitution, every faculty and function, including our mind, emotions, sexuality, conscience and will. In verses 13-17 there is a deliberate listing of different parts of the body. These bodily limbs and organs were created and given to us so that through them we might serve people and glorify God. Instead, they are used to harm people and in rebellion against God.

Third, the Old Testament quotations teach the universality of sin. No one is righteous, not even one. All have turned away from God. The repetition hammers home the point. The entire human race is in rebellion against God. There are no exceptions.

Every Mouth Speechless

ROMANS 3:19-20

> ¹⁹Now we know that whatever the law says, it says to those who are under the law, so that every mouth may be silenced and the whole world held accountable to God. ²⁰Therefore no one will be declared righteous in God's sight by the works of the law; rather, through the law we become conscious of our sin.

Jewish people reading the series of Old Testament quotations would assume that they applied to those wicked and lawless Gentiles. But Paul reminds Jews of their common knowledge: "we know that whatever the law says [here meaning the Old Testament in general], "it says to those who are under the law [literally *within* the law]," namely, themselves as Jews, so that they will be included in the judgment as well. In this way every mouth is stopped, every excuse silenced and the whole world, having been found guilty, is liable to God's judgment.

This is the point the apostle has been relentlessly moving to. The idolatrous and immoral Gentiles are "without excuse" (Romans 1:20). All critical moralists, whether Jews or Gentiles, equally "have no excuse" (Romans 2:1). The special status of the Jews does not exonerate them. In fact, all the inhabitants of the whole world, without any exception, are inexcusable before God. And by now the reason is plain. It is because all have known something of God and of morality (through Scripture in the case of the Jews, through nature in the case of the Gentiles), but all have disregarded and even stifled their knowledge in order to go their own way.

Romans 3:20 is the climax of Paul's argument, not just against Jewish self-confidence but against every attempt at self-salvation. For "through the law we become conscious of our sin." That is, what the law brings is the knowledge of sin, not the forgiveness of sin.

How should we respond to Paul's devastating exposure of universal sin and guilt? We should not try to evade it by changing the subject and talking instead of the need for self-esteem, or by blaming our behavior on our genes, nurturing, education or society. It is an essential part of our dignity as human beings that, however much we may have been affected by negative influences, we are not their helpless victims but rather responsible for our conduct.

Our first response to Paul's indictment should be to make certain that we have accepted this divine diagnosis of our human condition as true, and that we have fled from the just judgment of God on our sins to the only refuge there is, namely, Jesus Christ, who died for our sins. We have no merit to plead and no excuse to make. We too stand before God speechless and condemned. Only then shall we be ready to hear what follows, as Paul begins to explain how God has intervened through Christ and his cross for our salvation.

Righteousness from God

ROMANS 3:21-24

> [21]But now apart from the law the righteousness of God has been made known, to which the Law and the Prophets testify. [22]This righteousness is given through faith in Jesus Christ to all who believe. There is no difference between Jew and Gentile, [23]for all have sinned and fall short of the glory of God, [24]and all are justified freely by his grace through the redemption that came by Christ Jesus.

Romans 1:18–3:20 has presented a terrible picture of the human predicament. There was no flicker of hope, no prospect of rescue. "But now," Paul suddenly breaks in, God himself has intervened. A righteousness from God, apart from law, has been made known. Over against the unrighteousness of some and the self-righteousness of others, Paul sets the righteousness of God, which comes through faith in Jesus Christ to all who believe.

This righteousness is offered to all because it is needed by all. All *have* sinned, and all *continue* to fall short of the glory of God. God's "glory" could mean his approval or praise, which all have forfeited, but probably refers to his image or glory in which all were made but which all fail to live up to.

The righteousness of (or from) God is his just justification of the unjust, his righteous way of "righteousing" the unrighteous. *Justification* is a term belonging to the law courts. Its opposite is *condemnation*. Justification is not merely pardon.

Pardon is negative, the cancellation of a penalty or debt; justification is positive, the sinner's reinstatement in the favor and fellowship of God.

Further, sinners are justified through the redemption that came by Christ. *Redemption* is a commercial term borrowed from the marketplace. In the Old Testament it was used of slaves who were purchased in order to be set free. We were slaves or captives, in bondage to our sin and guilt, utterly unable to liberate ourselves. Jesus Christ redeemed us, bought us out of captivity, shedding his blood as the ransom price.

But how is it possible for the righteous God to declare the unrighteous to be righteous without either compromising his righteousness or condoning their unrighteousness? How can the righteous God act unrighteously? It would be unbelievable, if it were not for the cross of Christ. Without the cross, the justification of the unjust would be unjustified, immoral and therefore impossible. The only reason God justifies sinners is that Christ died for sinners. Because Christ shed his blood in a sacrificial death for us sinners, God is able justly to justify the unjust.

No formulation of the gospel is biblical that removes the initiative from God and attributes it either to us or even to Christ. It is certain that we did not take the initiative, for we were sinful, guilty and condemned, helpless and hopeless. Nor was the initiative taken by Jesus Christ in the sense that he did something that the Father was reluctant or unwilling to do. Christ came voluntarily and gave himself freely; yet he did it in submissive response to the Father's initiative.

Sacrifice of Atonement

ROMANS 3:25a

> [25]God presented Christ as a sacrifice of atonement,
> through the shedding of his blood—to be received by faith.

Another rendering of "sacrifice of atonement" is "propitiation."
Many Christians are embarrassed and even shocked by this word,
because to propitiate somebody means to placate his or her anger,
and it seems an unworthy concept of God (more pagan than
Christian) to suppose that he gets angry and needs to be ap-
peased. But we should not be shy of using the word *propitiation*
in relation to the cross, any more than we should drop the word
wrath in relation to God. Paul is describing God's solution to the
human predicament, which is not only sin but God's wrath upon
sin. And where there is divine wrath, there is the need to avert it.

Why is a propitiation necessary? The pagan answer is because
the gods are bad-tempered, subject to moods and fits, and capri-
cious. The Christian answer is because God's holy wrath rests on
evil. There is nothing unprincipled, unpredictable or uncontrolled about God's anger; it is aroused by evil alone.

Who undertakes to do the propitiating? The pagan answer is
that we do. We have offended the gods; so we must appease
them. The Christian answer, by contrast, is that we cannot
placate the righteous anger of God. We have no means whatever
by which to do so. But God in his undeserved love has done for
us what we could never do by ourselves. God *presented* Christ as
a sacrifice of atonement. The love, the idea, the purpose, the
initiative, the action and the gift were all God's.

How has the propitiation been accomplished? What is the propitiatory sacrifice? The pagan answer is that we have to bribe the gods with sweets, vegetable offerings, animals and even human sacrifices. The Old Testament sacrificial system was entirely different, since it was recognized that God himself gave the sacrifices to his people to make atonement. And this is clear beyond doubt in the Christian propitiation, for God gave his own Son to die in our place, and in giving his Son he gave himself. This is the basis on which the righteous God can "righteous" the unrighteous without compromising his own righteousness.

God Demonstrates His Righteousness

ROMANS 3:25b-26

[25]He did this to demonstrate his righteousness, because in his forbearance he had left the sins committed beforehand unpunished— [26]he did it to demonstrate his righteousness at the present time, so as to be just and the one who justifies those who have faith in Jesus.

The cross was a demonstration or public revelation as well as an achievement. It not only accomplished the propitiation of God and the redemption of sinners; it also vindicated the justice of God.

God left unpunished the sins of former generations, letting the nations go their own way and overlooking their ignorance, not because of injustice on his part or with any thought of condoning evil, but in his forbearance, and only because it was his intention in the fullness of time to punish these sins in the death of his Son. This was the only way in which he could simultaneously "be just," indeed "demonstrate his righteousness," and be "the one who justifies those who have faith in Jesus." Both justice (the divine attribute) and justification (the divine activity) would be impossible without the cross.

Through Christ's cross, God has redeemed his people, propitiated his wrath and demonstrated his justice. These three achievements belong together. Through the sin-bearing, substitutionary death of his Son, God has propitiated his own wrath in such a way as to redeem and justify us, and at the same time demonstrate his justice. We can only marvel at the wisdom, holiness, love and mercy of God, and fall down before him in humble worship. The cross should be enough to break the hardest heart and melt the iciest.

Three times in verses 22-26, Paul underlines the necessity of faith, the means by which we are justified. There is nothing meritorious about faith, and when we say that salvation is by faith, not by works, we are not substituting one kind of merit (faith) for another (works). Nor is salvation a cooperative enterprise between God and us, in which he contributes the cross and we contribute faith. The value of faith is not found in itself, but entirely and exclusively in its object, namely, Jesus Christ and him crucified. To say "justification by faith alone" is another way of saying "justification by Christ alone."

No other system, ideology or religion proclaims a free forgiveness and a new life to those who have done nothing to deserve it but have done a lot to deserve judgment instead. All other systems teach some form of self-salvation through good works of religion, righteousness or philanthropy. Christianity, by contrast, is not in its essence a religion at all; it is a gospel, *the* gospel, good news that God's grace has turned away his wrath, that God's Son has died our death and bore our judgment, that God has mercy on the undeserving, and that there is nothing left for us to do or even contribute. Faith's only function is to receive what grace offers.

Romans 3:9-26

....

Discussion Guide

Open

Bring to mind the largest financial debt you have ever had. Suppose you got a note from your creditor saying, "Someone else has paid your bill in full. You now owe nothing at all." What would you say and do?

Study

Read Romans 3:9–26.

1. Paul opens this section of his letter with the words "What shall we conclude then?" In view of verses 9-12, what is his conclusion about all that he has said thus far?

2. Focus on verses 13-18. What images do these words bring to your mind?

3. Notice the various parts of the body that Paul describes in verses 13-18. What impact does this have on the way you think about sin?

4. Verse 18 speaks of "fear of God." What kind of fear of God is appropriate?

5. How do you feel about seeing yourself described in the words of this passage?

6. According to verses 19-20, what is an appropriate response to the law?

7. Suppose someone said, "Since no one will be declared righteous by obeying God's law, why bother to pay any attention to it at all?" How would you respond?

8. Paul introduces a new section of Romans with the words "But now" (v. 21). What shift in emphasis do these words signal?

9. Verses 21-26 are tightly packed with a host of theological terms. Give the best definition you can for each of these: *righteousness*, *justified*, *grace*, *redemption*, *atonement*, *faith*. (A Bible dictionary or theological dictionary may help.)

10. Verse 22 says, "There is no difference." Find as many ways as you can in verses 21-26 that illustrate "no difference" between people.

11. Verse 24 says that we "are justified freely by his grace." What day-to-day impact does this have on you?

12. Paul opened his letter to the Romans with three and a half chapters on the topic of sin. What has this contributed to your view of yourself and your view of God?

13. How might these chapters affect your relationship to other people?

APPLY

1. Many people today do not like to use words like *right*, *wrong* and *sin*. They value personal freedom and believe that they should do whatever seems appropriate in a particular setting. In view of the first three chapters of Romans, how do you respond to this kind of thinking?

2. Some people feel constantly guilty, plagued by false guilt. Others seem guilt free, as if they have an inadequate sense of their own wrongdoing. But many people have a realistic view of personal sin. How would you describe your own sense of guilt and sin?

3. What hope would you offer someone who felt a constant nagging sense of guilt?

5

Romans 3:27–4:25
Forgive Us Our Debts

❧

Three Questions Answered

ROMANS 3:27-31

27Where, then, is boasting? It is excluded. Because of what law? The law that requires works? No, because of the law that requires faith. 28For we maintain that a person is justified by faith apart from the works of the law. 29Or is God the God of Jews only? Is he not the God of Gentiles too? Yes, of Gentiles too, 30since there is only one God, who will justify the circumcised by faith and the uncircumcised through that same faith. 31Do we, then, nullify the law by this faith? Not at all! Rather, we uphold the law.

Paul anticipates a fresh set of Jewish questions, related this time not to judgment but to justification, and in particular to justification by faith only.

What happens to boasting? All human beings are inveterate boasters. Boasting is the language of our fallen self-centeredness.

But in those who have been justified by faith, "boasting" is altogether "excluded." This is not on the principle of observing the law, which might give grounds for boasting, but on that of faith, which attributes salvation entirely to Christ and so eliminates all boasting. For our Christian conviction is that a sinner "is justified by faith," indeed by faith alone, "apart from the works of the law." Salvation is only by faith in Christ, which is why we should boast in him, not in ourselves. Praising, not boasting, is the characteristic activity of justified believers, and will be throughout eternity.

Is God the God of Jews only? Jewish people were extremely conscious of their special covenant relationship with God, in which Gentiles did not share. What the Jews forgot, however, was that their privileges were not intended for the exclusion of the Gentiles but for their ultimate inclusion when through Abraham's posterity all peoples on earth would be blessed. This covenant with Abraham has been fulfilled in Christ.

Do we nullify the law by this faith? Paul responds, "Not at all! Rather, we uphold the law." It seems most likely that Paul is defending himself against his critics who held that by declaring justification to be by faith, not obedience, Paul actively encouraged disobedience. This charge of antinomianism Paul will decisively refute in Romans 6–8. He anticipates these chapters here by the simple affirmation that faith upholds the law. What he means, and will later elaborate, is that justified believers who live according to the Spirit fulfill the righteous requirements of the law.

Here, then, are three implications—positive and negative—of the gospel of justification by faith alone. First, it humbles sinners and excludes boasting. Second, it unites believers and excludes discrimination. Third, it upholds the law and excludes antinomianism. No boasting. No discrimination. No antinomianism. This is the apostle's effective defense of the gospel against his critics.

Faith Credited as Righteousness

ROMANS 4:1-8

[handwritten note: freed by grace]

¹What then shall we say that Abraham, our forefather according to the flesh, discovered in this matter? ²If, in fact, Abraham was justified by works, he had something to boast about—but not before God. ³What does Scripture say? "Abraham believed God, and it was credited to him as righteousness."

⁴Now to the one who works, wages are not credited as a gift but as an obligation. ⁵However, to the one who does not work but trusts God who justifies the ungodly, their faith is credited as righteousness. ⁶David says the same thing when he speaks of the blessedness of the one to whom God credits righteousness apart from works:

⁷"Blessed are those

whose transgressions are forgiven,

whose sins are covered.

⁸Blessed is the one

whose sin the Lord will never count against them."

Paul's next step is to supply an Old Testament precedent and example. He chooses Abraham, Israel's most illustrious patriarch, supplemented by David, Israel's most illustrious king. He uses what Scripture says about them to elaborate the significance of both *justification*, in terms of the reckoning of righteousness to the unrighteous, and *faith*, in terms of trusting the God of creation and resurrection. Paul also wants Jewish Christians to grasp that his gospel of justification by faith is no novelty, having been proclaimed beforehand in the Old Testament, and he wants Gentile Christians to appreciate the rich spiritual heritage they have entered by faith in Jesus, in continuity with the Old Testament people of God.

Paul proceeds to draw out the significance of the verb *credited*, which he here uses for the first time. When used in a financial or commercial context, it signifies to put something to somebody's account. There are, however, two different ways that money can be credited to our account, namely, as wages (earned) or as a gift (free and unearned), and the two are necessarily incompatible. In the context of business, those who work have their wages credited to them as a right, for they have earned them. In the context of justification, however, to those who do not work and therefore have no right to payment but who instead put their trust in God who justifies the ungodly, "their faith is credited" to them "as righteousness," that is, they are given righteousness as a free and unearned gift of grace by faith.

Paul now moves on from Abraham to David. We notice at once how the language of "crediting" has changed. God is still the person who does the crediting, but now what he puts to our account is not "faith as righteousness" but "righteousness" itself. Instead of putting our sins into account against us, God pardons and covers them.

Paul's mind is not limited to one expression or to a single imagery. He has made it clear that the righteousness of (or from) God, which is revealed in the gospel, is God's just justification of the unjust. But when Paul affirms positively how God justifies the ungodly, he uses new expressions. First, God credits to us faith as righteousness. Second, he credits to us righteousness apart from works. And third, he refuses to credit our sins against us, but pardons and covers them instead. These three expressions are not precise synonyms, but they belong together in justification.

Justification involves a double counting, crediting or reckoning. On the one hand, negatively, God will never count our sins against us. On the other hand, positively, God credits our account with righteousness, as a free gift, by faith, altogether apart from our works.

Abraham Justified by Faith

ROMANS 4:9-12

[9]Is this blessedness only for the circumcised, or also for the uncircumcised? We have been saying that Abraham's faith was credited to him as righteousness. [10]Under what circumstances was it credited? Was it after he was circumcised, or before? It was not after, but before! [11]And he received circumcision as a sign, a seal of the righteousness that he had by faith while he was still uncircumcised. So then, he is the father of all who believe but have not been circumcised, in order that righteousness might be credited

to them. [12]And he is then also the father of the circumcised who not only are circumcised but who also follow in the footsteps of the faith that our father Abraham had before he was circumcised.

Paul's question has been whether Abraham was justified by works or by faith. Now he asks whether justification is available only for the circumcised (the Jews) or also for the uncircumcised (Gentiles). This question prompts another, concerning the circumstances in which Abraham was justified. Was he justified after he was circumcised or before? Did he submit to circumcision first, and so achieve righteousness, as the rabbis taught? Or was he already justified when he was circumcised? Paul's answer to his own question is brief and blunt: "It was not after, but before! In fact it happened long before."

Although the two events were separated, they were not unrelated. Abraham's circumcision, though not the ground of his justification, was its sign and seal. God himself had called circumcision the sign of the covenant he had established with Abraham. Paul now calls it a sign of his justification. As a sign it was a distinguishing mark, setting Abraham and his descendants apart as God's covenant people. Indeed, it was not only a "sign" to identify them; it was also a "seal" to authenticate them as the justified people of God.

Thus Abraham received two distinct gifts from God, justification and circumcision, in that order. First he received justification by faith while he was still uncircumcised. Second he received circumcision as a visible sign and seal of the justification that was already his.

"So then," Paul continues, there was a double purpose in the fact that Abraham was justified by faith and circumcised only later. It was first that Abraham might be "the father of all who believe," and so have been justified, "but have not been circumcised." In other words, Abraham is the father of Gentile believers. Circumcision is no more necessary to their justification than it was to his. The second purpose of this combination of faith, justification and circumcision was that Abraham might *also* be "the father of the circumcised who" in addition to their circumcision "also follow in the footsteps of the faith that our father Abraham had before he was circumcised." Thus he is the father of all believers, irrespective of whether they are circumcised or uncircumcised. In fact circumcision, which was of supreme importance to the Jews, must not be allowed to undermine or disrupt the unity of believers in Christ. For where circumcision divides, faith unites.

The Promise Comes by Faith

ROMANS 4:13-17

[13]It was not through the law that Abraham and his offspring received the promise that he would be heir of the world, but through the righteousness that comes by faith. [14]For if those who depend on the law are heirs, faith means nothing and the promise is worthless, [15]because the law brings wrath. And where there is no law there is no transgression.

[16]Therefore, the promise comes by faith, so that it may be by grace and may be guaranteed to all Abraham's offspring—not only to those who are of the law but also to

those who have the faith of Abraham. He is the father of us all. [17]As it is written: "I have made you a father of many nations." He is our father in the sight of God, in whom he believed—the God who gives life to the dead and calls into being things that were not.

Paul begins this new paragraph with a sharp "not . . . but" antithesis, in which the negative is emphatic. Now there are no questions and answers; there is just an uncompromising assertion that if justification is neither by works nor by circumcision, it is not by law either. For how did God's promise come to Abraham and his offspring? "Not through the law . . . but through the righteousness that comes by faith."

The promise Paul has in mind must be Genesis 15:5, that Abraham's posterity would be as numerous as the stars. It was a promise without any conditions or requirements attached to it. Abraham simply believed God and was justified.

Something can be given to us either by law or by promise, since God is the author of both, but they cannot be in operation simultaneously. Law and promise belong to different categories of thought, which are incompatible. Law language ("you shall") demands our obedience, but promise language ("I will") demands our faith. What God said to Abraham was not "Obey this law and I will bless you," but "I will bless you; believe my promise."

The words *law, transgression* and *wrath* belong to the same category of thought and language. For the law turns sin into transgression (a deliberate trespass), and transgression provokes God's wrath. Conversely, "where there is no law there is no transgression" and so no wrath. Paul then gives a further example of the logic of language, bringing together *grace* and *faith*. The fixed point is that God is gracious, and that salvation originates in his sheer grace alone. But in order that this may be so, our human response can only be faith. For grace gives and faith takes. Faith's exclusive function is humbly to receive what grace offers.

God's law makes demands, which we transgress, and so we incur wrath; God's grace makes promises, which we believe, and so we receive blessing. Thus law, obedience, transgression and wrath belong to one category of thinking, while grace, promise, faith and blessing belong to another.

Fully Persuaded

ROMANS 4:18-22

[18]Against all hope, Abraham in hope believed and so became the father of many nations, just as it had been said to him, "So shall your offspring be." [19]Without weakening in his faith, he faced the fact that his body was as good as dead— since he was about a hundred years old—and that Sarah's womb was also dead. [20]Yet he did not waver through unbelief regarding the promise of God, but was strengthened in his faith and gave glory to God, [21]being fully persuaded that God had power to do what he had promised. [22]This is why "it was credited to him as righteousness."

Before we are in a position to believe God's promises, we need to be sure both of his power (that he is able to keep them) and of his faithfulness (that he can be relied on to do so). These two attributes of God were the foundations of Abraham's faith. This firm conviction about the power of God was what enabled Abraham to believe, "against all hope" and "in hope" at the same time, when God promised him that his descendants would be as many as the stars, although at that time he and Sarah did not have even one child.

It is not that Abraham ran away from the realities of his situation into a world of fantasy. On the contrary, "without weakening in his faith," he faced the two painful, stubborn facts: that he could not beget a child and that Sarah could not conceive one. Yet out of that double death God brought a new life. It was at one and the same time an act of creation and of resurrection. For this is the kind of God Abraham believed in.

If Abraham had given in to unbelief, he would have "wavered" or been "at odds with himself." Instead, he strengthened himself by means of his faith. In this way he gave glory to God. That is, he glorified God by letting God be God and by trusting him to be true to himself as the God of creation and resurrection.

This concept of "letting God be God" forms a natural transition from God's power to his faithfulness. Whether people keep their promises or not depends not only on their power but also on their will to do so. Behind all promises lies the character of the person who makes them. Abraham knew this. As he contemplated his own great age and Sarah's barrenness, he neither turned a blind eye to these problems nor underestimated them. Instead, he reminded himself of God's power and faithfulness.

Faith always looks at the problems in the light of the promises. Abraham knew that God could keep his promises (because of his power) and he knew that he would do so (because of his faithfulness). It is because he believed God's promise, Paul concludes, that Abraham's faith was credited to him as righteousness.

Also for Us

Romans 4:23-25

> [23]The words "it was credited to him" were written not for him alone, [24]but also for us, to whom God will credit righteousness—for us who believe in him who raised Jesus our Lord from the dead. [25]He was delivered over to death for our sins and was raised to life for our justification.

Paul concludes this chapter by applying lessons from Abraham's faith to us, his readers. The whole Abraham story, like the rest of Scripture, was written for our instruction. Abraham was not unique in his experience of being justified by faith. For this is God's way of salvation for everybody.

But the God we are to trust in is not only the God of Abraham, Isaac and Jacob; he is also the God and Father of our Lord Jesus Christ, who "was delivered over to death for our sins and was raised to life for our justification." Thus both the death and the resurrection of Jesus are attributed to the Father's initiative.

In this chapter Paul gives us instruction about the nature of faith. He indicates that there are degrees in faith. Faith can be weak (v. 19) or strong (v. 20). How then does faith grow? Above all through the use of our minds. Faith is not burying our heads in the sand or screwing ourselves up to believe what we know is not true, or even whistling in the dark to keep our spirits up. On the contrary, faith is a reasoning trust. There can be no believing without thinking.

On the one hand, we have to think about the problems that face us. Abraham faced the reality of his apparently hopeless situation. On the other hand, he reflected on the promises of God and on the character of the God who had made them. And as his mind played on the promises, the problems shrank accordingly, for he was fully persuaded that God had power to do what he had promised.

We today are much more fortunate than Abraham and have little or no excuse for unbelief. For we live on this side of the resurrection. Moreover, we have a complete Bible in which both the creation of the universe and the resurrection of Jesus are recorded. It is therefore more reasonable for us to believe than it was for Abraham. Of course we have to make sure that the promises we are seeking to inherit are neither wrenched out of their biblical context nor the product of our own subjective fancy, but truly apply to us. Then we can lay hold of them, even "against all" human "hope," yet "in hope," that is, in the confidence of God's faithfulness and power. Only so will we prove to be genuine children of our great spiritual forefather Abraham.

Romans 3:27–4:25

Discussion Guide

Open

How do you react when you are around people who brag? What are you tempted to brag about?

Study

Read Romans 3:27–4:25.

1. What points of similarity does Paul find between Jews and Gentiles?

2. Why do we have no reason to boast (3:27)?

3. In what ways does the doctrine of justification by faith uphold the law (3:31)?

4. What words and phrases in Romans 4 seem most important to you? Why?

5. Why does Paul choose Abraham as his main example of justification?

6. Would you say that Abraham was justified by works or by faith? Explain your answer using information throughout Romans 4.

7. How does the quotation from David (vv. 7-8) back up Paul's case for justification by faith?

8. Romans 4:10 asks *when* Abraham was credited as righteous: after he was circumcised or before he was circumcised. What is the answer to that question, and what difference does it make (vv. 9-12)?

9. In what sense is Abraham "the father of us all" (v. 16)?

10. Reread verses 7-8, which come from Psalm 32:1-2. What is your own sense of blessing as you read those words?

11. God "gives life to the dead and calls into being things that were not" (v. 17). What examples do you see of this truth in verses 18-25?

APPLY

1. Jesus is alive (Romans 4:23-25). How does this fact affect who you are and what you want to become?

2. Pick a favorite sentence from somewhere in Romans 3–4. Meditate on it word by word. Why is the sentence significant to you?

4:25
r. 18

6

Romans 5:1-21
Peace with God

🌿

Certain Hope

ROMANS 5:1-5

¹Therefore, since we have been justified through faith, we have peace with God through our Lord Jesus Christ, ²through whom we have gained access by faith into this grace in which we now stand. And we boast in the hope of the glory of God. ³Not only so, but we also glory in our sufferings, because we know that suffering produces perseverance; ⁴perseverance, character; and character, hope. ⁵And hope does not put us to shame, because God's love has been poured out into our hearts through the Holy Spirit, who has been given to us.

The pursuit of peace is a universal human obsession, whether it is international, industrial, domestic or personal peace. Yet more fundamental than all these is peace with God, the reconciled relationship with him who is the first blessing of justification.

Through Christ we have gained access into grace. A better translation than "access" (which suggests that we take the initiative to enter) would be "introduction" (which acknowledges our unfitness to enter and our need for someone to bring us in). We have taken our stand firmly in or on this grace we have been introduced to.

Justified believers enjoy a blessing far greater than a periodic approach to God or an occasional audience with the king. We are privileged to live in the temple and in the palace. Our relationship with God, into which justification has brought us, is not sporadic but continuous, not precarious but secure. We do not fall in and out of grace like courtiers who may find themselves in and out of favor with their sovereign, or politicians with the public. No, we *stand* in it, for that is the nature of grace.

We also enjoy hope in God. Christian hope is not like our ordinary everyday hopes about the weather or our health; it is a joyful and confident expectation that rests on the promises of God. The object of our hope is "the glory of God," his radiant splendor that in the end will be fully displayed.

The fruits of our justification relate to the past, present and future. We have peace with God as a result of our past forgiveness. We are standing in grace, our present privilege. We rejoice in the hope of glory, our future inheritance. It sounds idyllic—except for Paul's fourth affirmation, that we rejoice in our sufferings.

These sufferings are literally *pressures*, referring to the opposition and persecution of a hostile world. Far from merely enduring these with stoic fortitude, we are to rejoice in them. This is not masochism; it is the recognition that there is a divine rationale behind suffering.

First, suffering is the one and only path to glory. It was so for Christ; it is so for Christians. Second, suffering can lead to maturity, if we respond to it positively and not with anger or bitterness. Third, suffering is the best context in which to become assured of God's love.

Paul has traced the sequence of chain reactions from tribulation to perseverance, from perseverance to character and from character to hope. Now he adds that hope will never betray us by proving to be illusory. What is the ultimate ground on which our Christian hope rests, our hope of glory? It is the steadfast love of God. The reason our hope will never let us down is that God will never let us down. His love will never give us up.

God Proves His Love

ROMANS 5:6-11

[6]You see, at just the right time, when we were still powerless, Christ died for the ungodly. [7]Very rarely will anyone die for a righteous person, though for a good person someone might possibly dare to die. [8]But God demonstrates his own love for us in this: While we were still sinners, Christ died for us.

[9]Since we have now been justified by his blood, how much more shall we be saved from God's wrath through him! [10]For if, while we were God's enemies, we were reconciled to him through the death of his Son, how much more, having been reconciled, shall we be saved through

his life! [11]Not only is this so, but we also boast in God through our Lord Jesus Christ, through whom we have now received reconciliation.

Previously Paul wrote that God demonstrated his justice on the cross (Romans 3:25-26). Now he sees the cross as a demonstration of God's love. Indeed, *demonstrate* is too weak a word; *prove* would be better.

The more a gift costs the giver and the less the recipient deserves it, the greater the love is seen to be. Measured by these standards, God's love in Christ is unique. In sending his Son to die for sinners, he gave everything, his very self, to those who deserved nothing from him except judgment.

Human beings can be very generous toward those they consider worthy of their affection and respect. The unique majesty of God's love is that God (1) gave himself, (2) even to the horrors of a sin-bearing death on the cross and (3) did so for his undeserving enemies. How, then, can we doubt the love of God?

Verses 9 and 10 are notable examples of the familiar New Testament tension between the *already* and the *not yet*, between what Christ has accomplished at his first coming and what remains to be done at his second, between our past and our future salvation. We have been saved through Christ from the guilt of our sins and from the judgment of God, but we have not yet been delivered from indwelling sin or been given new bodies in the new world. So the best is yet to be! In our present condition we eagerly look forward to our full and final salvation.

But how can we be sure of it? Here is the logic. If God has already done the difficult thing, can we not trust him to do the comparatively simple thing of completing the task? If God has accomplished our justification at the cost of Christ's blood, "much more" will he save his justified people from his final wrath! If he reconciled us to himself when we were his enemies, "much more" will he finish our salvation now that we are his reconciled friends!

Therefore we "boast" or "exult" in God. To exult in God is to rejoice not in our privileges but in his mercies, not in our possession of him but in his of us.

It is clear from Paul's writing that the major mark of justified believers is joy, especially joy in God himself. We should be the most positive people in the world. For the new community of Jesus Christ is characterized not by self-centered triumphalism but by God-centered worship.

Because All Sinned

ROMANS 5:12-14

> [12]Therefore, just as sin entered the world through one man, and death through sin, and in this way death came to all people, because all sinned—
>
> [13]To be sure, sin was in the world before the law was given, but sin is not charged against anyone's account where there is no law. [14]Nevertheless, death reigned from the time of Adam to the time of Moses, even over those who did not sin by breaking a command, as did Adam, who is a pattern of the one to come.

"Therefore," Paul continues. What follows is not an alien intrusion into the argument or an isolated unconnected section or even a parenthesis, but a logical development, a conclusion of his thesis thus far and a necessary transition to what comes next.

Paul begins with the topic of sin and death. He describes three downward steps or deteriorating stages in human history, from one man sinning to all people dying.

First, "sin entered the world through one man." Adam is not named but is obviously meant. Paul is not concerned with the origin of evil in general, but only with how it invaded the world of human beings. It entered through one man, that is, through his disobedience.

Second, "death" then entered the world "through sin." As Adam was the door through which sin entered, so sin was the door through which death entered.

Third, "in this way death came to all people, because all sinned." The apostle is still handling the relation between sin and death, but now he moves on from their presence in "one man" to their presence in "all people" (the human race). Moreover, he sees a similarity between these two situations ("in this way"). He may refer to the essential connection between sin and death: as death came to one man because he sinned, so death came to all people because they sinned. Or he may refer to the agency through which both happened: as through one man sin and death entered the world, so through one man they spread throughout the world.

Until the Mosaic law was given and could exercise its role of defining and identifying sin, sin was not reckoned against sinners. "Nevertheless, death reigned" throughout the period before the law was given, "even over those who did not sin by breaking a [specific, explicit] command." Of course some did flagrantly disobey God's moral law, which was written in their hearts. But Paul's point is that there were others who did not disobey any direct commands of God. Yet all died (the reference is clearly to physical death), and death is the penalty for sin. All died "because all sinned" in and through Adam, the representative of the human race.

Determined as he is to honor Jesus Christ as the only mediator of all our blessings, Paul will present Adam and Christ, the respective heads of the old and new humanities, in such a way as to demonstrate the overwhelming superiority of the work of Christ.

Trespass and Gift Contrasted

ROMANS 5:15-17

> [15]But the gift is not like the trespass. For if the many died by the trespass of the one man, how much more did God's grace and the gift that came by the grace of the one man, Jesus Christ, overflow to the many! [16]Nor can the gift of God be compared with the result of one man's sin: The judgment followed one sin and brought condemnation, but the gift followed many trespasses and brought justification. [17]For if, by the trespass of the one man, death reigned through that one man, how much more will those who receive God's abundant provision of grace and of the gift of righteousness reign in life through the one man, Jesus Christ!

Paul has called Adam the type or prototype of Christ. But he has no sooner made this statement than he feels embarrassed by the unseemliness of what he has said. Certainly there is a superficial similarity between Christ and Adam: each is one man through whose one deed enormous numbers of people have been affected. But there the likeness ends. How can the Lord of glory be likened to the man of shame, the Savior to the sinner, the giver of life to the broker of death? The correspondence is not a parallel but an antithesis. So before returning to the sole similarity between them, Paul elaborates their dissimilarities.

First, the nature of their actions was different. Adam's "trespass" was a fall, indeed "the fall," a deviation from the path that God had clearly shown him. He insisted on going his own way. Paul contrasts Christ's "gift," an act of self-sacrifice that bears no resemblance to Adam's act of self-assertion.

Second, the immediate effect of their actions was different. In the case of Adam, God's judgment brought condemnation; in the case of Christ, God's gift brought justification. Yet there is more to the antithesis than the two words *condemnation* and *justification*. God's judgment "followed" only "one sin," whereas God's gift "followed many trespasses." The secular mind would expect many sins to attract more judgment than one sin. But grace operates a different arithmetic.

Third, the ultimate effect of the two actions is also different. Once more "the one man" Adam and "the one man Jesus Christ" are juxtaposed, and so are the end results of their actions, which now are said to be "death" and "life." But this time the contrast highlights the superiority of the work of Christ. On the one hand, we are given the stark information that "death reigned," not now temporarily from Adam to Moses but permanently. On the other hand, we are not told that through Christ "life reigned." The words "how much more" alert us to expect a greater blessing. The recipients of God's abundant grace will themselves "reign in life."

Formerly death was our king, and we were slaves under its totalitarian tyranny. Christ has not merely exchanged death's kingdom for the gentler kingdom of life, while leaving us in the position of subjects. Instead, he delivers us from the rule of death so radically that we change places with it and rule over it or "reign in life." We become kings and queens, sharing the kingship of Christ. Even death is under our feet now, and one day death will be destroyed.

Just as . . . So Also

ROMANS 5:18-19

> [18]Consequently, just as one trespass resulted in condemnation for all people, so also one righteous act resulted in justification and life for all people. [19]For just as through the disobedience of the one man the many were made sinners, so also through the obedience of the one man the many will be made righteous.

Having completed his contrast between Adam and Christ, Paul now develops the comparison. His "just as . . . so also" structure is intended to highlight the similarity between Adam and Christ. The one act of the one man determined the destiny of the many.

Paul takes up the immediate results of the work of Adam and Christ, namely, condemnation and justification. His emphasis is on the parallel: "just as" one trespass resulted in condemnation, "so also" one righteous act resulted in justification and life. Paul then takes up the nature of their actions, though using different language from verse 15. There it was trespass and gift; here it is disobedience and obedience. Yet the emphasis is on the parallel that "just as" through Adam's disobedience many were made sinners, "so also" through Christ's obedience many will be made righteous. The expressions "made sinners" and "made righteous" cannot mean that these people actually became morally good or evil, but rather that they were constituted legally righteous or unrighteous in God's sight.

The parallel between Adam and Christ has led a number of Bible students to conclude that Paul taught universalism, that the life won by Christ will be as universal as the death caused by Adam. One argument universalists use is that the expressions "the many" and "all people" appear to be synonymous and therefore interchangeable. But we have no liberty to insist that the word *all* is invariably absolute and can never admit any qualification, for Scripture itself often uses it relatively of all within a certain category or context, or from a particular perspective.

Nevertheless, this passage of Romans gives us solid grounds for confidence that a very large number will be saved and that the scope of Christ's redeeming work, although not universal, will be extremely extensive. This expectation should be a great spur to world evangelization. For God's promise assures us that the church's mission will be attended by great blessing and that a mighty harvest is yet to be reaped. We are not told exactly how God will achieve this result. All we know is that we are to preach the gospel to all nations, and that God's grace will triumph in the end.

Grace Reigns

ROMANS 5:20-21

[20]The law was brought in so that the trespass might increase. But where sin increased, grace increased all the more, [21]so that, just as sin reigned in death, so also grace might reign through righteousness to bring eternal life through Jesus Christ our Lord.

Paul has been developing his analogy between Adam and Christ. His Jewish readers may have been asking if there was any room in his scheme for Moses. What was the purpose of the law? Paul says that it was "brought in so that the trespass might increase." Part of what Paul meant by this he has already explained in previous places. The law reveals sin, defining and displaying it (Romans 3:20). The law turns sin into transgression, since "where there is no law there is no transgression" (Romans 4:15). In Romans 7:8 Paul will add that the law even provokes sin. These statements must have shocked Jewish people, who thought of the Mosaic law as having been given to increase righteousness, not to increase sin. Yet Paul says that the law increased sin rather than diminishing it and provoked sin rather than preventing it.

God, however, had made ample provision for the increase of sin by the increase of his grace. This allusion to grace introduces Paul's third comparison between Adam and Christ, in which he takes up the alternative ultimate issues of life and death. Verse 21 contains no explicit mention of Adam, but he lurks behind it in the reference to sin and death. Once more the contrasts are not forgotten, as grace and life are set in antithesis to sin and death.

But the emphasis is on the parallel which compares two kinds of "reign." God's purpose is that "just as sin reigned in death, so also grace might reign through righteousness to bring eternal life."

Nothing could better sum up the blessings of being in Christ than the expression "the reign of grace." Grace forgives sins through the cross and bestows on the sinner both righteousness and eternal life. Grace satisfies the thirsty soul and fills the hungry with good things. Grace sanctifies sinners, shaping them into the image of Christ. Grace perseveres even with the recalcitrant, determining to complete what it has begun. And one day grace will destroy death and consummate the kingdom. So when we are convinced that grace reigns, we will remember that God's throne is a throne of grace, and we will come to it boldly to receive mercy and to find grace for every need.

Romans 5:1-21

....

Discussion Guide

Open

Describe one of your favorite mental pictures of peace.

Study

Read Romans 5:1-21.

1. Pick a phrase or sentence in Romans 5:1-11 that you particularly appreciate. Why are these words significant to you?

2. How does your attitude toward suffering compare with the attitude Paul advocates?

3. Why can we rejoice even in our suffering (v. 3)?

4. Verses 3-5 describe a sequence that begins with suffering and ends with hope—with several stages in between. When have you seen that sequence in yourself or in someone else?

5. Describe the work of Christ as seen in verses 6-11.

6. Consider the way Paul portrays those for whom Christ died (vv. 6-8). In what ways do you qualify to be included in his description?

7. Paul uses the word *reconciliation* in verse 11. In view of his letter thus far, what does he mean by this term?

8. Romans 5:12-17 speaks of Adam and of Jesus Christ. What impact did each have on the human race? (Find all the examples that you can.)

9. Notice the repeated pattern of "just as . . . so also." What comparisons does this phrase highlight?

10. What is the difference between the Jewish boasting in God, which Paul mentions in Romans 2:17, and the Christian boasting in God he writes about in Romans 5:11?

11. Which of the two forms of boasting typically characterizes your life?

12. What does it mean to you that believers will "reign in life" (v. 17)?

13. Where and how do you most need the assurance of peace with God?

APPLY

1. What do you hope for in the future?

2. To what extent do your hopes include what Paul has in mind in this passage?

7

Romans 6:1-23

United to Christ and Enslaved to God

Buried and Risen with Christ

ROMANS 6:1-4

¹What shall we say, then? Shall we go on sinning so that grace may increase? ²By no means! We are those who have died to sin; how can we live in it any longer? ³Or don't you know that all of us who were baptized into Christ Jesus were baptized into his death? ⁴We were therefore buried with him through baptism into death in order that, just as Christ was raised from the dead through the glory of the Father, we too may live a new life.

In his concentration on the secure status of the people of God, Paul has said little or nothing about Christian life or growth or discipleship. He seems to have jumped straight from justification to glorification, without any intervening stage of sanctification. Already his critics have slanderously misquoted him as saying, "Let us do evil that good may result" (Romans 3:8). Now Paul refutes their slander.

Paul's answer to his critics is that God's grace not only forgives sins but also delivers us from sinning. For grace does more than justify; it also sanctifies. Paul does not declare the literal impossibility of sin in believers but rather the moral incongruity of it.

We died to sin. How can we live in what we have died to? It is important to note that Paul is not referring to a minority of exceptionally holy Christians. He is describing all Christians, who have believed and been baptized into Christ. Whatever this death to sin may be, it is common to all Christian people. Are all God's people dead to sin in the sense of being unresponsive to it? No; scriptural and historical biographies, together with our own experience, all deny this. Our fallen nature is so alive and active that we are urged not to obey its desires and are given the Holy Spirit to subdue and control them.

Instead, the way in which we have died to sin is that our baptism united us with Christ in his death. Baptism signifies our union with Christ, especially with Christ crucified and risen. Union with Christ by faith, which is invisibly accomplished by the Holy Spirit, is visibly signified and sealed by baptism. Those who ask whether Christian people are free to sin betray their complete ignorance of what their baptism meant.

The essential point Paul is making is that being a Christian involves a personal, vital identification with Jesus Christ, and that this union with him is dramatically set forth in our baptism. The death and resurrection of Jesus Christ are not only historical facts and significant doctrines, but also personal experiences, since through faith-baptism we have come to share in them ourselves. We were "baptized into his death" and we were "buried with him through baptism into death," so that "just as Christ was raised from the dead through the glory of the Father, we too may live a new life," Christ's resurrection life, which begins now and will be completed on the day of our own resurrection.

No Longer Slaves

ROMANS 6:5-7

> [5]For if we have been united with him in a death like his, we will certainly also be united with him in a resurrection like his. [6]For we know that our old self was crucified with him so that the body ruled by sin might be done away with, that we should no longer be slaves to sin—[7]because anyone who has died has been set free from sin.

Paul tells us that something happened, in order that something else might happen, in order that a third thing might happen. "Our old self was crucified with" Christ, "so that the body ruled by sin might be done away with, that we should no longer be slaves to sin." The best way to grasp Paul's logic is to take these three stages in the opposite order. God's end purpose is our freedom from sin's tyranny. But before our rescue is possible, "the body ruled by sin" must be "done away with."

This *body* is certainly not the physical human body. The biblical doctrines of creation, incarnation and resurrection all give us a high view of our body as the God-intended vehicle we express ourselves through. Rather it is the body dominated by sin, because sin uses our body for its own evil purposes. It is our former self, the person we used to be in Adam. What was crucified with Christ was not a part of us called our old nature but the whole of us as we were in our preconversion state.

The only way to be justified from sin is that the wages of sin are paid, either by the sinner or by the God-appointed substitute. How can a person be justified who has been convicted of a crime and sentenced to a term of imprisonment? Only by going to prison and paying the penalty of the crime. Once the sentence is served, the person can leave prison justified.

The same principle holds good if the penalty is death. You may respond that in this case to pay the penalty is no way of escape. And you would be right if we were talking about capital punishment on earth. But the wonderful thing about our Christian justification is that our death is followed by a resurrection, in which we can live the life of a justified person, having paid the death penalty (in and through Christ) for our sin.

We deserved to die for our sins. And in fact we did die, not in our own person but in the person of Jesus Christ our substitute, who died in our place and with whom we have been united by faith and baptism. By union with the same Christ we have risen again. So the old life of sin is finished, because we died to it, and the new life of justified sinners has begun.

Our death and resurrection with Christ render it inconceivable that we should go back. It is in this sense that our sinful self has been deprived of power and we have been set free.

Alive with Christ

ROMANS 6:8-10

[8]Now if we died with Christ, we believe that we will also live with him. [9]For we know that since Christ was raised from the dead, he cannot die again; death no longer has mastery over him. [10]The death he died, he died to sin once for all; but the life he lives, he lives to God.

Commentators are divided as to whether the verb *will live* in verse 8 is logical (future in relation to the death which preceded it) or chronological (future in relation to the present moment). If it is logical, it refers to our sharing Christ's life now; if it is chronological, it refers to our sharing his resurrection on the last day. It is doubtful, however, whether Paul would have conceived of either without the other. Life is resurrection anticipated; resurrection is life consummated.

The guarantee of the continuing nature of our new life, beginning now and lasting forever, is found in Christ's resurrection. "For we know that since Christ was raised from the dead, he cannot die again." He was not resuscitated, brought back to this life, in which case like Lazarus he would have had to die again. Instead he was resurrected, raised to an altogether new plane of living, from which there will never be any question of return. "Death no longer has mastery over him." Having been delivered from its tyranny, he has passed beyond its jurisdiction forever.

Next Paul summarizes the death and resurrection of Jesus that he has been writing about. Although he implies that the two realities belong together and must never be separated, he also indicates that there are radical differences between them. There is a difference of time (the past event of death, the present experience of life), of nature (he died to sin, bearing its penalty, but lives to God, seeking his glory) and of quality (the death "once for all," the resurrection life continuous). These differences are important for our understanding not only of the work of Christ but also of our Christian discipleship, which, by our union with Christ, begins with a once-for-all death to sin and continues with an unending life of service to God. Our old life terminated with the judicial death it deserved; our new life began with a resurrection.

Offer Yourselves to God

ROMANS 6:11-14

> [11]In the same way, count yourselves dead to sin but alive to God in Christ Jesus. [12]Therefore do not let sin reign in your mortal body so that you obey its evil desires. [13]Do not offer any part of yourself to sin as an instrument of wickedness, but rather offer yourselves to God as those who have been brought from death to life; and offer every part of yourself to him as an instrument of righteousness. [14]For sin shall no longer be your master, because you are not under the law, but under grace.

We have died to sin and risen to God. We must therefore "count" or "reckon" ourselves "dead to sin but alive to God" in, or by reason of, our union with, "Christ Jesus." This reckoning is not make-believe. Paul does not call us to pretense but to reflection and recollection. We are to recall, to ponder, to grasp, to register these truths until they are so integral to our mindset that a return to the old life is unthinkable.

Regenerate Christians should no more contemplate a return to unregenerate living than adults to their childhood, married people to their singleness or released prisoners to their prison cells. Our union with Jesus Christ has severed us from the old life and committed us to the new. Our baptism stands between the two like a door between two rooms, closing on the one and opening into the other. We have died, and we have risen. How can we possibly live again in what we have died to?

Paul's exhortation has negative and positive aspects that complement one another. Do not offer yourselves "to sin," he says, because you have died to it; instead offer yourselves "to God," because you have risen to live for his glory. "Therefore do not let sin reign in your mortal body so that you obey its evil desires." Paul's use of the adjective *mortal* shows that he means our physical body. Its "parts" are likely to be our various limbs and organs (eyes and ears, hands and feet), although probably including our human faculties or capacities, which can be used by sin as "instruments of wickedness." Paul next exhorts us to the positive alternative: "rather offer yourselves to God" because you "have been brought from death to life." Since we have died to sin, it is inconceivable that we should let sin reign in us or offer ourselves to it. Since we are alive to God, it is only appropriate that we should offer ourselves and our faculties to him.

The apostle supplies a further reason for offering ourselves not to sin but to God. It is that "sin shall no longer be your master." This is not a command but an assurance, even a promise. Why will sin no longer be your master? "Because you are not under the law, but under grace." To be "under the law" is to accept the obligation to keep it and so to come under its curse or condemnation. To be "under grace" is to acknowledge our dependence on the work of Christ for salvation, and so to be justified rather than condemned, and thus to be set free.

Slaves to Righteousness

ROMANS 6:15-18

> [15]What then? Shall we sin because we are not under the law but under grace? By no means! [16]Don't you know that when you offer yourselves to someone as obedient slaves, you are slaves of the one you obey—whether you are slaves to sin, which leads to death, or to obedience, which leads to righteousness? [17]But thanks be to God that, though you used to be slaves to sin, you have come to obey from your heart the pattern of teaching that has now claimed your allegiance. [18]You have been set free from sin and have become slaves to righteousness.

We think of Roman slaves as either captured in war or bought in the marketplace. But there was such a thing as voluntary slavery, in which impoverished people enslaved themselves simply for food and housing. Such voluntary slaves could not expect to give themselves to a slave master and simultaneously retain their freedom. It is the same with spiritual slavery. Self-surrender leads inevitably to slavery, "whether" we become "slaves to sin, which leads to death, or to obedience, which leads to righteousness."

As the alternative to being "slaves to sin," we might expect "slaves to Christ" rather than "slaves to obedience"; and as the alternative to "death," we might expect "life" rather than "righteousness." Yet the idea of being "obedient to obedience" is a dramatic way of emphasizing that obedience is the very essence of slavery, and "righteousness" in the sense of justification is almost a synonym of life. Conversion is an act of self-surrender; self-surrender leads inevitably to slavery; and slavery demands total, radical, exclusive obedience. Once we have offered ourselves to Christ, we are permanently and unconditionally at his disposal.

So complete is the change that has taken place in the Roman Christians' lives that Paul breaks out into a spontaneous doxology: "Thanks be to God!" He then sums up their experience in four stages, which concern what they used to be, what they did, what happened to them and what they had become.

First, "you used to be slaves to sin." All human beings are slaves, and there are only two slaveries, to sin and to God. Conversion is a transfer from the one to the other.

Second, "you have come to obey from your heart the pattern of teaching that has now claimed your allegiance." This is an unusual description of conversion. The Roman Christians are said to have obeyed not God or Christ, but a certain pattern or standard of teaching. This must have been the apostolic instruction, which probably included both gospel doctrine and personal ethics. Paul evidently sees conversion not only as trusting in Christ but as believing and acknowledging the truth.

Third, the Romans "have been set free from sin," emancipated from its slavery. They have not become perfect, but they have been decisively rescued out of the lordship of sin into the lordship of God, out of the dominion of darkness into the kingdom of Christ.

Fourth, in consequence they "have become slaves to righteousness." So decisive is this transfer by the grace and power of God from the slavery of sin to the slavery of righteousness that Paul cannot restrain himself from thanksgiving.

The Gift of God

ROMANS 6:19-23

> [19]I am using an example from everyday life because of your human limitations. Just as you used to offer yourselves as slaves to impurity and to ever-increasing wickedness, so now offer yourselves as slaves to righteousness leading to holiness. [20]When you were slaves to sin, you were free from the control of righteousness. [21]What benefit did you reap at that time from the things you are now ashamed of? Those things result in death! [22]But now that you have been set free from sin and have become slaves of God, the benefit you reap leads to holiness, and the result is eternal life. [23]For the wages of sin is death, but the gift of God is eternal life in Christ Jesus our Lord.

Paul begins with an apology for the human terms he uses to describe conversion, for slavery is not an altogether accurate or appropriate metaphor of the Christian life. Then why did the

apostle use it? "Because of your human limitations." His readers'
weakness must be a reference to their fallenness, either in their
minds, so that they are dull of perception, or in their characters,
so that they are vulnerable to temptation and need to be reminded of the obedience they have committed themselves to.

In spite of his apologetic explanation, Paul continues to
compare and contrast the two slaveries. But this time he draws
an analogy between them in the way they both develop. Both
are dynamic, the one steadily deteriorating, the other steadily
progressing. Despite the antithesis between them, an analogy is
drawn between the grim process of moral deterioration and the
glorious process of moral transformation.

Each slavery is also a kind of freedom, one authentic, the
other spurious. Similarly, each freedom is a kind of slavery, although one is degrading and the other ennobling. The way to
assess the rival claims of these two slaveries or freedoms is by
evaluating their benefit, literally their "fruit." The negative benefits of slavery to sin and freedom from righteousness are remorse in the present (a sense of guilt over "the things you are
now ashamed of") and in the end "death," the eternal death of
separation from God in hell. "But now," the positive benefits of
freedom from sin and slavery to God are "holiness" in the present
and in the end "eternal life," surely meaning fellowship with
God in heaven. Thus there is a freedom that spells death, and
there is a bondage that spells life.

There is a further contrast between the terms of service on
which the two slave owners operate. Sin pays wages (you get
what you deserve), but God gives a free gift (you are given what

you do not deserve). If we are determined to get what we deserve, it can only be death; by contrast, eternal life is God's gift, wholly free and utterly undeserved. The only ground on which this gift is bestowed is the atoning death of Christ, and the only condition of receiving it is that we are "in Christ Jesus our Lord," that is, personally united to him by faith.

Romans 6:1-23

....

DISCUSSION GUIDE

OPEN

When you hear the words *slave* or *slavery*, what do you think of?

STUDY

Read Romans 6:1-23.

1. How might Paul's gospel seem to stimulate people to sin more than ever?

2. What is Paul's answer to this objection?

3. In what various ways are the words *dead* and *alive* used in verses 1-14?

4. How are we united with Christ in his death?

5. How are we united with Christ in his resurrection?

6. When have you experienced a sense of being united with the living Christ?

7. In a practical sense, what does it mean to be dead to sin?

8. Identify several contrasts between the two forms of slavery: slavery to sin and slavery to Christ.

9. When have you observed the benefits (one negative, one positive) of the two forms of slavery?

10. Why does slavery to sin offer a false sense of freedom?

11. What are some ways that you struggle with allowing sin to have dominion in your physical body?

12. How does this passage from Romans offer you encouragement?

APPLY

1. What are some ways you can remind yourself to count or reckon yourself as dead to sin and alive with Christ?

2. Put at least one of those ways into practice this week.

8

Romans 7:1-25
Battling Sin

❧

A Marriage Metaphor

ROMANS 7:1-3

¹Do you not know, brothers and sisters—for I am speaking to those who know the law—that the law has authority over someone only as long as that person lives? ²For example, by law a married woman is bound to her husband as long as he is alive, but if her husband dies, she is released from the law that binds her to him. ³So then, if she has sexual relations with another man while her husband is still alive, she is called an adulteress. But if her husband dies, she is released from that law and is not an adulteress if she marries another man.

Paul turns to the question of the purpose of God's law. What is the place of the law in Christian discipleship now that Christ has come and inaugurated the new era? In Romans 7 he will deal with three possible attitudes to the law. We can call them legalism, antinomianism and law-fulfilling freedom. Paul rejects the first two and commends the third. Legalists fear the law and are in bondage to it. Antinomians hate the law and repudiate it. Law-abiding free people love the law and fulfill it.

The dominant theme of the first part of Paul's argument is release from the law. Paul lays down the principle that the law has authority over a person only while the person is alive. Death brings release from all contractual obligations involving the dead person. If death supervenes, relationships established and protected by law are terminated. Death changes not only the obligations of the dead person (which are obviously canceled) but also the obligations of anyone who had a contract with the dead person.

As an example of this general principle, Paul chooses marriage. By law a married woman is bound to her husband as long as he lives, but if her husband dies she is released from that law of marriage. The contrast is clear: the law binds her, but his death frees her. Moreover, her release is complete.

"So then," Paul now draws a conclusion, "if she [the married woman] has sexual relations with another man while her husband is still alive, she is called an adulteress. But if her husband dies," and she remarries, she "is not an adulteress," because she has been "released from that law" which had previously bound her.

What has made the difference? How is it that one remarriage would make her an adulteress, while the other would not? Of course the answer lies in her husband's death. The second marriage is morally legitimate because death has terminated the first. Only death can secure freedom from the marriage law and therefore the right to remarry. These references to death, freedom from law and remarriage already hint at the application Paul is about to make.

Released from the Law

ROMANS 7:4-6

> 4So, my brothers and sisters, you also died to the law
> through the body of Christ, that you might belong to an-
> other, to him who was raised from the dead, in order that
> we might bear fruit for God. 5For when we were in the
> realm of the flesh, the sinful passions aroused by the law
> were at work in us, so that we bore fruit for death. 6But now,
> by dying to what once bound us, we have been released
> from the law so that we serve in the new way of the Spirit,
> and not in the old way of the written code.

Paul turns from human laws to the law of God. It too claims lordship over us while we live. Without explicitly saying so, the apostle implies that we were previously married to the law and so under its authority. But as death terminates a marriage contract and permits remarriage, so we "also died to the law through the body of Christ," *so that we* "might belong to another."

The purposes of our dying with Christ to the law are now spelled out. The immediate purpose is that we belong to "him who was raised from the dead." The result of being released from the law and joined to Christ is holy living, for becoming a Christian involves a radical change of allegiance.

Paul draws a sharp distinction between the old covenant, which was one of an external code written on stone tablets, and the new covenant, which is one of the Spirit. The new age is essentially the age of the Spirit, in which the Holy Spirit writes God's law in our hearts.

What has caused this release from the old life and this introduction to the new? It is that radical double event called death and resurrection. We "died to the law" through the death of Christ; now we belong to Christ, having been "raised from the dead" with him.

So we return to the question of whether the law is still binding on Christians and whether we are still expected to obey it. Yes and no! Yes, in the sense that Christian freedom is freedom to serve, not freedom to sin. We are still slaves, slaves of God and of righteousness. But also no, because the motives and means of our service have completely changed.

Why do we serve? Not because the law is our master and we have to, but because Christ is our master and we want to. Not because obedience leads to salvation but because salvation leads to obedience. And how do we serve? "In the new way of the Spirit." For the indwelling of the Holy Spirit is the distinguishing characteristic of the new age, and so of the new life in Christ.

Sin Seizes the Opportunity

ROMANS 7:7-11

⁷What shall we say, then? Is the law sinful? Certainly not! Nevertheless, I would not have known what sin was had it

not been for the law. For I would not have known what
coveting really was if the law had not said, "You shall not
covet." [8]But sin, seizing the opportunity afforded by the
commandment, produced in me every kind of coveting.
For apart from the law, sin was dead. [9]Once I was alive
apart from the law; but when the commandment came, sin
sprang to life and I died. [10]I found that the very commandment that was intended to bring life actually brought
death. [11]For sin, seizing the opportunity afforded by the
commandment, deceived me, and through the commandment put me to death.

In his treatment of the law, Paul performs a skillful balancing
act. He is neither wholly positive nor wholly negative toward the
law, but ambivalent. On the one hand, the law is indeed the law
of God, the revelation of his righteous will. On the other hand,
the law is unable to save sinners, and its impotence is a major
reason for every continuing inner conflict.

Must the law be dubbed "sinful" in the sense that it is responsible for creating sin? After his emphatic rejoinder "Certainly
not!" the apostle begins to delve into the relations between the
law and sin.

First, the law reveals sin. Paul has already written that
"through the law we become conscious of our sin" (Romans 3:20).
Now he writes, "I would not have known what sin was had it not
been for the law." This probably means both that he had come
to recognize the gravity of sin, because the law unmasks and
exposes it as rebellion against God, and that he had been brought
under conviction of sin by it.

Second, the law provokes sin. Sin establishes within us a base or foothold by means of the commandments that provoke us. This provocative power of the law is a matter of everyday experience. Ever since Adam and Eve, human beings have always been enticed by forbidden fruit. The real culprit is not the law but sin, which is hostile to God's law. We cannot blame the law for proclaiming God's will. Sin twists the function of the law from revealing, exposing and condemning sin into encouraging and even provoking it.

Third, the law condemns sin. To explain this further, Paul first repeats that "sin" seized "the opportunity afforded by the commandment" and adds that sin first "deceived me" (presumably by promising blessings it could not deliver) and then "through the commandment put me to death."

Here, then, are the three devastating effects of the law in relation to sin. It exposes, provokes and condemns sin. But the law is not in itself sinful, nor is it responsible for sin. Instead, sin itself, our sinful nature, uses the law to cause us to sin and so to die. The law is exonerated; sin is to blame.

That Sin May Be Recognized

ROMANS 7:12-13

¹²So then, the law is holy, and the commandment is holy, righteous and good.

¹³Did that which is good, then, become death to me? By no means! Nevertheless, in order that sin might be recognized as sin, it used what is good to bring about my

death, so that through the commandment sin might become utterly sinful.

The requirements of God's law are both holy and righteous in themselves and also good. Yet verse 10 seems to implicate the law as being responsible for death, stating that the commandment which "was intended to bring life actually brought death."

So was the law guilty of offering life with one hand and inflicting death with the other? The apostle emphatically answers, "By no means!" The law does not cause sin; it exposes and condemns it. And the law does not cause death; sin does. But "in order that sin might be recognized as sin, it used what is good [that is, the law] to bring about my death, so that [this was God's intention] through the commandment sin might become utterly sinful." The extreme sinfulness of sin is seen precisely in the way it exploits a good thing (the law) for an evil purpose (death).

Suppose a criminal is caught red-handed breaking the law. He is arrested, brought to trial, found guilty and sentenced to prison. He cannot blame the law for his imprisonment. The law convicted and sentenced him, but he has no one to blame but himself and his own criminal behavior.

In a similar way, Paul exonerates the law. The villain is indwelling sin which, because of its perversity, is aroused and provoked by the law. The antinomians, who say that our whole problem is the law, are quite wrong. Our real problem is not the law but sin. Indwelling sin accounts for the weakness of the law, as the apostle will go on to show. The law cannot save us because we cannot keep it, and we cannot keep it because of indwelling sin. At the same time, God's law remains holy, righteous and good.

The Desire but Not the Deed

ROMANS 7:14-20

[14]We know that the law is spiritual; but I am unspiritual, sold as a slave to sin. [15]I do not understand what I do. For what I want to do I do not do, but what I hate I do. [16]And if I do what I do not want to do, I agree that the law is good. [17]As it is, it is no longer I myself who do it, but it is sin living in me. [18]For I know that good itself does not dwell in me, that is, in my sinful nature. For I have the desire to do what is good, but I cannot carry it out. [19]For I do not do the good I want to do, but the evil I do not want to do—this I keep on doing. [20]Now if I do what I do not want to do, it is no longer I who do it, but it is sin living in me that does it.

Paul proclaims the impotence of the law by dramatizing it in the vivid terms of personal experience. He writes almost exactly the same things twice, presumably for emphasis.

Paul begins with a frank acknowledgment of innate sinfulness. "We know" and "I know." In both cases the self-knowledge concerns the flesh. Those who are still under the law love it (because they are regenerate), yet they are enslaved (because they are also fallen) and so are incapable of turning good desires into good deeds.

After confessing that he does not understand his own actions, and that he has desires for good that he cannot carry out, the apostle summarizes his inward struggle in negative and positive counterparts. He is conscious of a divided "I." There is an "I" that wants the good and hates the evil, and there is an "I" that does what is hated and does not do what is wanted. The conflict is between desire and performance; the will is there, but the ability is not. His whole being (especially his mind and will) is set upon God's law. He wants to obey it. When he sins, it is against his reason, his desire, his consent. But the law cannot help him. Only the power of the indwelling Spirit could change things.

Then who is to blame for the good I do not do and the evil I do? It is not the law, for Paul declares its holiness and goodness. But neither am "I myself" responsible, the authentic "I." For when I do evil, I do not do it voluntarily. On the contrary, I act against my better judgment, my will and my consent. It is rather "sin living in me," the false, the fallen, the counterfeit "I." The real I, "I myself," is the "I" that loves and wants the good and hates the evil, for that is its essential orientation. Therefore the "I" that does the opposite is not the real or the genuine "I," but rather a usurper, "my sinful nature." In other words, the law is neither responsible for our sinning nor capable of saving us. It has been fatally weakened by the sinful nature.

Thanks Be to God, Who Delivers

ROMANS 7:21-25

21So I find this law at work: Although I want to do good, evil is right there with me. 22For in my inner being I delight in God's law; 23but I see another law at work in me, waging war against the law of my mind and making me a prisoner of the law of sin at work within me. 24What a wretched man I am! Who will rescue me from this body that is subject to death? [25]Thanks be to God, who delivers me through Jesus Christ our Lord!

So then, I myself in my mind am a slave to God's law, but in my sinful nature a slave to the law of sin.

Having given a graphic description of inward conflict, as he identifies with believers under the law, Paul now summarizes the situation in terms of their double reality. He depicts this double reality four times in four different ways: as two egos, two laws, two cries and two slaveries.

First, there are two egos. What Paul writes might be paraphrased: "When in me there is a desire to do good, then by me evil is close at hand." The evil and the good are both present simultaneously, for they are both part of a fallen yet regenerate personality.

Second, there are two laws. The characteristic of "the law of my mind" is that it operates "in my inner being" and "delights in God's law," whereas the characteristic of "the law of sin" is that it is "at work within me," fighting against the law of my mind and "making me a prisoner." This is the condition of the person who is still under the law.

Third, there are two cries from the heart. One is "What a wretched man I am! Who will rescue me from this body that is subject to death?" The other is "Thanks be to God, who delivers me through Jesus Christ our Lord!" The first is a cry of longing that ends in a question mark, while the second is a cry of confidence and thanksgiving that ends in an exclamation mark. Yet both are the cries of the same person who is a regenerate believer, who laments his corruption, who yearns for the final deliverance at the resurrection, who knows the impotence of the law to rescue him and who exults in God through Christ as the only Savior.

Fourth, there are two slaveries. "I myself [the authentic, re-generate I] in my mind am a slave to God's law," for I know it and love it and want it, "but in my sinful nature [my false and fallen self, uncontrolled by the Spirit] [I am] a slave to the law of sin," on account of my inability by myself to keep it. The conflict is between my renewed mind and my unrenewed nature.

We need to keep a watch on ourselves and others, lest we should ever slip back from the new order into the old, from a person to a system, from freedom to slavery, from the indwelling Spirit to an external code, from Christ to the law.

Romans 7:1-25

....

Discussion Guide

Open

When you hear the term *the law of God*, what are some of your reactions?

Study

Read Romans 7:1-25.

1. What legal changes happen to a wife when her husband dies (vv. 1-3)?

2. What similar changes happen when we die to the law (vv. 4-6)?

3. Does this mean that Christians do not keep a moral code? (Use this passage as a basis for your answer.)

4. Focus on verses 7-13. Find everything you can about what is good about the law.

5. In these same verses, what limitations do you see to what the law can accomplish?

6. What influence has God's law had on you?

7. Focus on verses 14-25. What makes this person a "wretched man"?

8. What examples of this kind of struggle have you seen in your own life?

9. Paul says in verse 18, "I have the desire to do what is good, but I cannot carry it out." What does this imply about a person's relationship with God?

10. In spite of this conflict, why is Paul thankful (vv. 24-25)?

APPLY

Paul addresses three approaches to God's law: legalism (you have to obey it), antinomianism (you just ignore it) and law-fulfilling freedom (you don't count on keeping the law to make you right with God, but you love God's law and enjoy following it).

1. Which best describes your own current relationship with God's law?

2. If this is different from some other stage of your life, what caused the change?

9

Romans 8:1-17
Rescued by God's Spirit

❦

Justified and Liberated

ROMANS 8:1-2

> [1]Therefore, there is now no condemnation for those who are in Christ Jesus, [2]because through Christ Jesus the law of the Spirit who gives life has set you free from the law of sin and death.

In Romans 8, Paul paints the essential contrast between the weakness of the law and the power of the Spirit. Over against indwelling sin, which is the reason the law is unable to help us in our moral struggle, Paul sets the indwelling Spirit, who is both our liberator now from "the law of sin and death" and the guarantee of resurrection and eternal glory in the end. Thus the Christian life is essentially life in the Spirit, a life that is animated, sustained, directed and enriched by the Holy Spirit. Without the Holy Spirit, true Christian discipleship would be inconceivable, indeed impossible.

The word *therefore* indicates that the apostle is summing up his argument thus far about salvation through the death and resurrection of Christ. The word *now* emphasizes that this salvation is already ours if we are in Christ.

The first blessing of salvation is expressed in the words *no condemnation*, which are equivalent to *justification*. Paul will go on to explain that our not being condemned is due to God's action of condemning our sin in Christ. Our justification, together with its corresponding truth of "no condemnation," is securely grounded in what God has done for us in and through Jesus Christ.

The second privilege of salvation is expressed in the next statement: "because through Christ Jesus the law of the Spirit who gives life has set you free from the law of sin and death." Thus "liberation" joins "no condemnation" as the two great blessings that are ours if we are "in Christ Jesus." These two blessings are linked by the conjunction *because*, indicating that our liberation is the basis of our justification. It is because we have been liberated that no condemnation can overtake us.

What have we been set free from? From "the law of sin and death." The context demands that this is a description of God's law, the Torah. Shocking as it may sound, God's holy law could be called "the law of sin and death" because it occasioned both. To be liberated from the law of sin and death through Christ is to be no longer under the law, that is, to give up looking to the law for either justification or sanctification.

The means of our liberation Paul calls "the law of the Spirit who gives life." This must mean the gospel. The gospel has freed us from the law and its curse, and the message of life in the Spirit has freed us from the slavery of sin and death. This liberation has been Paul's own experience. It is also the experience of every believer in Christ.

Spirit Empowerment

ROMANS 8:3-4

> ³For what the law was powerless to do because it was weakened by the flesh, God did by sending his own Son in the likeness of sinful flesh to be a sin offering. And so he condemned sin in the flesh, ⁴in order that the righteous requirement of the law might be fully met in us, who do not live according to the flesh but according to the Spirit.

The law could neither justify nor sanctify because it was "weakened by the flesh," that is, our fallen selfish nature. But what the sin-weakened law could not do, "God did." He made provision for both our justification and our sanctification. He sent his Son, whose incarnation and atonement are alluded to in verse 3. Then he gave us his Spirit, through whose indwelling power we are enabled to fulfill the law's requirement.

Paul unfolds what "God did" in five expressions.

First, God sent "his own Son." The statement that it was his own Son indicates that the Son enjoyed a prior life of intimacy with the Father. It certainly expresses the Father's sacrificial love in sending him.

Second, the sending of the divine Son involved his becoming incarnate, a human being, expressed by the words "in the likeness of sinful flesh." The Son's humanity was simultaneously both real and sinless.

Third, God sent his Son "to be a sin offering." As "in the likeness of sinful flesh" is clearly an allusion to the incarnation, "to be a sin offering" clearly refers to the atonement.

Fourth, God "condemned sin in the flesh," that is, in the humanity of Jesus. God judged our sins in the sinless humanity of his Son, who bore them in our place. The law condemns sin, in the sense of expressing disapproval of it, but when God condemned sin in his Son, God's judgment fell upon sin in the sinless Christ.

Fifth, God sent his own Son and condemned our sin in him so that "the righteous requirement of the law might be fully met in us." Law-abiding Christian behavior is the ultimate purpose of God's action through Christ. "Righteous requirement" refers to the commandments of the moral law as a whole, which God wants to be "fully met" in his people. The law can be fulfilled only in those who live "according to the Spirit." The flesh renders the law impotent, but the Spirit empowers us to obey it.

Holiness is Christlikeness, and Christlikeness is fulfilling the righteousness of the law. The end God had in view when he sent his Son was not only our justification, through freedom from the condemnation of the law, but also our holiness, through obedience to the commandments of the law. Although law obedience is not the ground of our justification, it is the fruit of it and the very meaning of sanctification.

Holiness is the work of the Holy Spirit. Romans 7 insists that we cannot keep the law because of our indwelling sinful nature; now Romans 8:4 insists that we can and must because of the indwelling Spirit. Holiness is the fruit of trinitarian grace, of the Father sending his Son into the world and his Spirit into our hearts.

The Mind of the Spirit

ROMANS 8:5-8

> [5]Those who live according to the flesh have their minds set on what the flesh desires; but those who live in accordance with the Spirit have their minds set on what the Spirit desires. [6]The mind governed by the flesh is death, but the mind governed by the Spirit is life and peace. [7]The mind governed by the flesh is hostile to God; it does not submit to God's law, nor can it do so. [8]Those who are in the realm of the flesh cannot please God.

Paul now develops an antithesis between the mind, or mindset, of those who are characterized by the flesh and those who are characterized by the Spirit. His purpose is to explain why obedience to the law is possible only to those who live according to the Spirit.

Our mindset expresses our basic nature as Christians or non-Christians. Paul's meaning is not that people are like this because they think like this, but that they think like this because they *are* like this. Their nature determines their mindset.

Our mindset is a matter of what preoccupies us, the ambitions that drive us and the concerns that engross us, how we spend our time and our energies, what we concentrate on and give ourselves up to. All this is determined by who we are, whether we are still governed by the flesh or are now by new birth governed by the Spirit.

Our mindset has eternal consequences. The mindset of flesh-dominated people is already one of spiritual death and leads inevitably to eternal death, for it alienates them from God and renders fellowship with him impossible in either this world or the next. The mindset of Spirit-dominated people, however, entails life and peace. On the one hand they are alive to God, alert to spiritual realities and thirsty for God like nomads in the desert. On the other hand they have peace with God, peace with their neighbor and peace within, enjoying an inner integration or harmony. We would more eagerly pursue holiness if we were convinced that it is the way of life and peace.

Our mindset concerns our fundamental attitude to God. The reason the mind of the flesh is death is that it is "hostile to God," cherishing a deep-seated animosity against him. It is antagonistic to his name, kingdom and will, to his day, his people and his word, to his Son, his Spirit and his glory. In contrast to the regenerate, who delight in God's law, the unregenerate mind "does not submit to God's law, nor can it do so," which explains why those who live according to the flesh cannot fulfill the law's righteous requirement.

Here are two categories of people (the unregenerate, who are in the flesh, and the regenerate, who are in the Spirit), who have two perspectives or mindsets (the mind of the flesh and the mind of the Spirit), which lead to two patterns of conduct (living according to the flesh or the Spirit) and result in two spiritual states (death or life, enmity or peace). Our mind, where we set it and how we occupy it, plays a key role in both our present conduct and our final destiny.

The Spirit Who Lives in You

ROMANS 8:9-11

> [9]You, however, are not in the realm of the flesh but are in the realm of the Spirit, if indeed the Spirit of God lives in you. And if anyone does not have the Spirit of Christ, they do not belong to Christ. [10]But if Christ is in you, then even though your body is subject to death because of sin, the Spirit gives life because of righteousness. [11]And if the Spirit of him who raised Jesus from the dead is living in you, he who raised Christ from the dead will also give life to your mortal bodies because of his Spirit who lives in you.

Every true Christian has received the Spirit, so that our body has become a temple of the Holy Spirit. If we do not have Christ's Spirit in us, we do not belong to Christ at all. This makes it plain that the gift of the Spirit is an initial and universal blessing, received when we first repent and believe in Jesus. Of course there may be many further and richer experiences of the Spirit and many fresh anointings of the Spirit for special tasks, but the personal indwelling of the Spirit is every believer's privilege from the beginning.

The body is "subject to death," which means that it is mortal, destined to die. Yet in the midst of our physical mortality, our spirits are alive in Christ. What is the cause of this double condition, a dying body and a living spirit? The answer lies in the repeated "because," which attributes death to sin and life to righteousness. Since Paul has already made this attribution in his Adam-Christ parallelism in chapter 5, he must be saying that our bodies became mortal because of Adam's sin, whereas our spirits are alive because of Christ's righteousness, that is, because of the righteous standing he has secured for us.

The ultimate destiny of our body is not death, however, but resurrection. Christ's resurrection is the pledge and the pattern of our own resurrection. The same Spirit who raised him will also raise us. This does not mean that our dead bodies will be resuscitated and restored to their present material existence, only to die again. No, resurrection includes transformation, the raising and changing of our body into a new and glorious vehicle of our personality, and its liberation from all frailty, disease, pain, decay and death.

Already we express our personality through our body, especially by speech, but also by posture and gesture, by a look in our eyes or an expression on our face. We even call it "body language." But the language that our present body speaks is imperfect; we easily miscommunicate. In the new body, there will be a perfect correspondence between message and medium, between what we want to communicate and how we do so. The resurrection body will be the perfect vehicle of our redeemed personality.

A Spiritual Obligation

ROMANS 8:12-13

   12Therefore, brothers and sisters, we have an obligation—but it is not to the flesh, to live according to it. 13For if you

> live according to the flesh, you will die; but if by the Spirit
> you put to death the misdeeds of the body, you will live.

Paul introduces the neglected topic of *mortification*, the process of putting to death the body's misdeeds. This is neither masochism (taking pleasure in self-inflicted pain) nor asceticism (resenting and rejecting the fact that we have bodies and natural bodily appetites). Rather it is a clear-sighted recognition of evil as evil, leading to such a decisive and radical repudiation of it that no imagery can do it justice except "putting to death."

What we are to "put to death" is "the misdeeds of the body," that is, every use of our body that serves ourselves instead of God and other people. Note that it is something that *we* have to do. It is not a question of dying or of being put to death, but of "putting to death." In the work of mortification we are not passive, waiting for it to be done to us or for us. On the contrary, we are responsible for putting evil to death. True, Paul immediately adds that we can do this only "by the Spirit," by his agency and power. For only he can give us the desire, determination and discipline to reject evil. Nevertheless, it is we who must take the initiative to act.

Negatively, we must totally repudiate everything we know to be wrong. If temptation comes to us through what we see, handle or visit, then we must be ruthless in not looking, not touching, not going, and so in controlling the approaches of sin. Positively, we are to set our minds on the things the Spirit desires, set our hearts on things above and occupy our thoughts with what is noble, right, pure and lovely.

To engage in mortification, we need strong motives. One is that "we have an obligation" to the indwelling Spirit of life.

Another is that the death of mortification is the only road to life. Verse 13 contains the most marvelous promise: "you will live." Paul seems to allude to the life of God's children, who are led by his Spirit and assured of his fatherly love. This rich, abundant, satisfying life can be enjoyed only by those who put their misdeeds to death. The pain of mortification is worthwhile if it opens the door to fullness of life.

So we need to redefine both life and death. What the world calls life (a desirable self-indulgence) leads to alienation from God, which in reality is death. The putting to death of all perceived evil within us, which the world sees as an undesirable self-abnegation, is in reality the way to authentic life.

Heirs of God

ROMANS 8:14-17

> [14]For those who are led by the Spirit of God are the children of God. [15]The Spirit you received does not make you slaves, so that you live in fear again; rather, the Spirit you received brought about your adoption to sonship. And by him we cry, *"Abba*, Father." [16]The Spirit himself testifies with our spirit that we are God's children. [17]Now if we are children, then we are heirs—heirs of God and co-heirs with Christ, if indeed we share in his sufferings in order that we may also share in his glory.

This paragraph concerns the witness the Spirit bears us, that is, the assurance he gives us that we are God's children. Precisely how is the Spirit's witness borne? Paul assembles four pieces of evidence.

First, the Spirit leads us into holiness. The topic, which continues from verse 13, is still the sanctifying work of the Holy Spirit. The new, rich, full life, which is enjoyed by those who put their misdeeds to death, is precisely the experience of being God's children. As such we are granted a specially close, personal, loving relationship with our heavenly Father, immediate and bold access to him in prayer, membership of his worldwide family, and nomination as his heirs.

Second, the Spirit replaces fear with freedom in our relationship to God. Paul uses the imagery of slavery and freedom to contrast our pre- and postconversion situations. The slavery of the old age led to fear, especially of God as our judge; the freedom of the new age gives us boldness to approach God as our Father.

Third, the Spirit prompts us in our prayers to call God "Father." When we cry, "Abba! Father!" we experience the inward witness of the Holy Spirit that we are children of God. Paul did not mean that the two witnesses, our spirit and the Holy Spirit, are equal, but that the Holy Spirit bears a strong inward witness *to* our spirit that we are God's children.

Fourth, the Spirit is the firstfruits of our inheritance. At first sight this seems to refer to that heavenly inheritance which God is keeping in heaven for us. It is possible, however, that the inheritance Paul has in mind is not something God intends to bestow on us, but *God himself*. As for the further astonishing statement that we are also "co-heirs with Christ," we recall that Jesus himself prayed that his own might be with him and might see his glory and share his love.

There is a qualification, however: "if indeed we share in his sufferings." Scripture emphasizes that suffering is the path to glory. It was so for the Messiah; it is so for the messianic community. The essence of discipleship is union with Christ, which means identification with him in both his sufferings and his glory.

There is no indication here that the witness of the Holy Spirit is a special, distinctive or overwhelming experience that should be sought by all but is given only to some. On the contrary, the whole paragraph is descriptive of what is, or should be, common to all believers. Though doubtless in differing degrees of intensity, all who have the Spirit's indwelling are given the Spirit's witness too.

Romans 8:1-17

....

Discussion Guide

Open

When and how have you seen God's kindness?

Study

Read Romans 8:1-17.

1. According to verses 1-4, what all has God done?

2. In what different ways might people respond to these actions by God?

3. How have you responded at various stages of your life?

4. In spite of having written seven chapters about sin and our inability to keep God's law, Paul now writes, "Therefore, there is now no condemnation." How can he write this?

5. Focus on verses 5-8. How is a mind "set on what the flesh desires" different from a mind "set on what the Spirit desires"?

6. Drawing on the information in verses 9-11, what do you learn about the Holy Spirit?

7. What do the same verses reveal about the Trinity?

8. Focus on verses 12-17. What do you enjoy in these verses? Why?

9. What further work of the Holy Spirit do you see in these verses?

10. What effect does it have on you that you can speak to God as "Father"?

Apply

1. What are some ways that you can show your appreciation for being adopted into God's family?

2. The Christian life is essentially life in the Spirit, a life that is animated, sustained, directed and enriched by the Holy Spirit. Without the Holy Spirit, true Christian discipleship would be inconceivable and indeed impossible. In view of all that this passage reveals about the Holy Spirit, how can you give appropriate attention to his presence in your life?

10

Romans 8:18-39
Present Pain, Future Glory

❦

Creation Liberated

ROMANS 8:18-21

¹⁸I consider that our present sufferings are not worth comparing with the glory that will be revealed in us. ¹⁹For the creation waits in eager expectation for the children of God to be revealed. ²⁰For the creation was subjected to frustration, not by its own choice, but by the will of the one who subjected it, in hope ²¹that the creation itself will be liberated from its bondage to decay and brought into the freedom and glory of the children of God.

Paul moves on from the present ministry of God's Spirit to the future glory of God's children. Clearly what prompts this development is his previous allusion to our sharing in the sufferings and glory of Christ.

The sufferings include not only the opposition of the world but our physical and moral human frailty, which is due to our

provisional, half-saved condition. The glory, however, is the un-
utterable splendor of God, eternal, immortal and incorruptible.
The magnificence of God's revealed glory will greatly surpass the
unpleasantness of our sufferings.

The sufferings and glory of the old creation (the material
order) and of the new (the people of God) are integrally related
to each other. Both creations are suffering and groaning now;
both are going to be set free together. As nature shared in the
curse and now shares in the pain, so it will also share in the glory.
"The creation waits in eager expectation" for the revelation of
God's children, that is, the disclosure of their identity and their
investiture with glory. This will be the signal for the renewal of
the whole creation.

Paul writes that the creation "was subjected to frustration."
This reference must be to the judgment of God that fell on the
natural order following Adam's disobedience. The basic idea of
frustration is emptiness, whether of purpose or of result. Creation's subjection to frustration was "not by its own choice, but by
the will of the one who subjected it, in hope." Only God, being
both Judge and Savior, entertained hope for the world he cursed.

God has promised that creation's subjection to frustration will
not last forever. One day it will experience a new beginning, which
Paul terms a liberation from its bondage to decay. *Decay* denotes not
only that the universe is running down, but that nature is enslaved,
locked into an unending cycle, where conception, birth and growth
are relentlessly followed by decline, decay, death and decomposition.
Creation still works, for the mechanisms of nature are fine-tuned
and delicately balanced. And much of it is breathtakingly beautiful,

revealing the Creator's hand. But it is also in bondage to disintegration and frustration.

In the end, however, creation will be "liberated . . . into the freedom and glory of the children of God." Nature will be brought out of bondage into freedom, out of decay into glory, that is, out of corruption into incorruption. Indeed, God's creation will share in the glory of God's children, which is itself the glory of Christ.

Patient and Eager

ROMANS 8:22-27

> [22]We know that the whole creation has been groaning as in the pains of childbirth right up to the present time. [23]Not only so, but we ourselves, who have the firstfruits of the Spirit, groan inwardly as we wait eagerly for our adoption to sonship, the redemption of our bodies. [24]For in this hope we were saved. But hope that is seen is no hope at all. Who hopes for what they already have? [25]But if we hope for what we do not yet have, we wait for it patiently.
>
> [26]In the same way, the Spirit helps us in our weakness. We do not know what we ought to pray for, but the Spirit himself intercedes for us through wordless groans. [27]And he who searches our hearts knows the mind of the Spirit, because the Spirit intercedes for God's people in accordance with the will of God.

Even while the creation eagerly awaits the final revelation, it is "groaning" in pain. Its groans are neither meaningless nor symptoms of despair. Rather, they are like "the pains of child-birth," for they provide assurance of the coming emergence of a new order. Not only is the whole creation groaning, but "we ourselves . . . groan inwardly." Caught in the tension between what God has inaugurated (by giving us his Spirit) and what he will consummate (in our final adoption and redemption), we groan with discomfort and longing. The indwelling Spirit gives us joy, and the coming glory gives us hope, but the interim suspense gives us pain.

Though we have not yet received our final adoption or redemption, we have already received the Holy Spirit as both foretaste and promise of these blessings. The presence of the Spirit is a constant reminder of the incompleteness of our salvation, as we share with the creation in the frustration, the bondage to decay and the pain. We groan because of our physical frailty and mortality. However, it is not only our fragile body that makes us groan; it is also our fallen nature, which hinders us from behaving as we should, and would altogether prevent us from it, if not for the indwelling Spirit.

Just as the groaning creation waits eagerly for God's children to be revealed, so we groaning Christians wait eagerly for our adoption, even our bodily redemption. Of course we have already been adopted by God, and the Spirit assures us that we are his children. Yet there is an even deeper and richer child-Father relationship to come when we are fully revealed as God's children and conformed to the likeness of his Son. We were saved in hope of our total liberation, just as the creation was subjected to frustration in hope of being set free from it.

As we live between present difficulty and future destiny, between the already and the not yet, the correct Christian posture is that of waiting "eagerly," with keen expectation, and waiting "patiently," steadfast in the endurance of our trials. We are to wait neither so eagerly that we lose our patience, nor so patiently that we lose our expectation, but eagerly and patiently together.

In this in-between state, the Holy Spirit helps our weakness when we pray. Our infirmity is our ignorance: "We do not know what we ought to pray for." But the Spirit knows what we do not know. He intercedes for us, and does so with speechless groans. The Holy Spirit identifies with our groaning, with the pain of the world and the church, and shares in the longing for the final freedom of both.

God Works for Our Good

ROMANS 8:28

> [28]And we know that in all things God works for the good of those who love him, who have been called according to his purpose.

Romans 8:28 is surely one of the best-known texts in the Bible. Believers of every age and place have stayed their minds on it. It has been likened to a pillow on which to rest our weary heads.

The sentence begins with the assertion that "we know." There are many things we do not know. In those areas in which God has not plainly revealed his mind, our correct attitude is one of Christian agnosticism. But here Paul lists five truths about God's providence that "we know."

First, we know that "God works," or is at work, in our lives. The order of words permits the translation "we know that for those who love God he is working." He is ceaselessly, energetically and purposefully active on our behalf.

Second, God is at work "for the good of" his people. Being himself wholly good, his works are all expressions of his goodness and are calculated to advance his people's good. Moreover, the "good" that is the goal of all his providential dealings with us is our ultimate well-being, namely, our final salvation.

Third, God works for our good "in all things." *All things* must include the sufferings of verse 17 and the groanings of verse 23. Nothing is beyond the overruling, overriding scope of God's providence.

Fourth, God works in all things for the good of "those who love him." This is a necessary limitation. Paul is not expressing a general, superficial optimism that everything tends to everybody's good in the end. No, if the "good" that is God's objective is our completed salvation, then its beneficiaries are his people who are described as those who love him. This is an unusual phrase for Paul, because his references in Romans to love are rather to God's love for us. Nevertheless, elsewhere he does allude to our love for God, and this is a common biblical concept, since the first and great commandment is that we love God with all our being.

Fifth, those who love God are also described as those "who have been called according to his purpose." They love him because he first loved them, and his love finds expression in his eternal purpose and his historical call. So life is not the random mess it sometimes appears to be. God has a saving purpose and is working in accordance with it.

We do not always understand what God is doing, let alone welcome it. Nor are we told that he is at work for our comfort. But we know that in all things he is working toward our supreme good.

Conformed to Christ's Image

ROMANS 8:29-30

> [29]For those God foreknew he also predestined to be conformed to the image of his Son, that he might be the firstborn among many brothers and sisters. [30]And those he predestined, he also called; those he called, he also justified; those he justified, he also glorified.

Paul traces God's good and saving purpose through five stages: foreknowledge, predestination, calling, justification and glorification.

First comes a reference to "those God foreknew." Since the common meaning of "to foreknow" is to know something beforehand, some conclude that God foresees who will believe, and that this foreknowledge is the basis of his predestination. But this cannot be right. God foreknows everybody and everything, whereas Paul is referring to a particular group. Also, if God predestines people because they are going to believe, then the ground of their salvation is in themselves and their merit, instead of in him and his mercy.

Second, those God foreknew "he also predestined to be conformed to the image of his Son." Clearly a decision is involved in the process of becoming a Christian, but it is God's decision before it can be ours. This is not to deny that we decided for Christ, and freely, but to affirm that we did so only because he had first decided for us. Paul singles out two practical purposes of God's predestination. The first is that we should "be conformed to the image of his Son." God's eternal purpose for his people is that we should become like Jesus. The transformation process begins here and now, but it will be brought to completion only when Christ returns. The second purpose is that, as a result of our conformity to the image of Christ, "he might be the firstborn among many brothers and sisters," enjoying both the community of the family and the preeminence of the firstborn.

Paul's third affirmation is that "those he predestined, he also called." God's call comes to people through the gospel. When the gospel is preached to them with power, and they respond to it with the obedience of faith, then we know God has chosen them. What Paul means by God's call is not the general gospel invitation but the divine summons that raises the spiritually dead to life.

Fourth, "those he called, he also justified." God's effective call enables those who hear it to believe, and those who believe are justified by faith. Justification is more than forgiveness or acquittal or even acceptance; it is a declaration that we sinners are now righteous in God's sight because of his conferment on us of a righteous status, which is the righteousness of Christ himself.

Finally, "those he justified, he also glorified." Paul has already promised that if we share Christ's sufferings we will share his glory and that the creation itself will one day be brought into the freedom of the glory of God's children. Now he uses the verb *glorified.* Our destiny is to be given new bodies in a new world, both of which will be transfigured with the glory of God.

Five Unanswerable Questions

ROMANS 8:31-36

[31]What, then, shall we say in response to these things? If God is for us, who can be against us? [32]He who did not spare his own Son, but gave him up for us all—how will he not also, along with him, graciously give us all things? [33]Who will bring any charge against those whom God has chosen? It is God who justifies. [34]Who then is the one who condemns? No one. Christ Jesus who died—more than that, who was raised to life—is at the right hand of God and is also interceding for us. [35]Who shall separate us from the love of Christ? Shall trouble or hardship or persecution or famine or nakedness or danger or sword? [36]As it is written:

"For your sake we face death all day long;
we are considered as sheep to be slaughtered."

Paul hurls five questions into space and challenges anybody and everybody, in heaven, earth or hell, to answer them and to deny the truth they contain. To understand the significance of these questions, it is essential to grasp why each remains unanswered: because of a truth that is either contained in the question or attached to it by an "if" clause. The clearest example is the first.

"If God is for us, who can be against us?" If Paul had simply asked, "Who is against us?" there would immediately have been a barrage of replies. For we have formidable foes arrayed against us. But the situation Paul envisions is one in which "God is for us," since he has foreknown, predestined, called, justified and glorified us. This being so, who can be against us?

"He who did not spare his own Son, but gave him up for us all—how will he not also, along with him, graciously give us all things?" How can we possibly be sure that God will supply all our needs? The way Paul phrases his question banishes these doubts. For he points us to the cross. The God of whom we ask whether or not he will give us all things is the God who has already given us his Son. The cross is the guarantee of the continuing, unfailing generosity of God.

"Who will bring any charge against those whom God has chosen?" If the question "Who will accuse us?" stood on its own, many voices would be raised in accusation. Our conscience accuses us. Our accuser the devil never ceases to press charges against us. We also have human enemies who delight to point an accusing finger at us. But none of their allegations can be sustained. God has chosen us and has justified us. Therefore all accusations fall to the ground.

"Who then is the one who condemns?" Christ died for the sins we would deservedly be condemned for. After death he "was raised to life" by the Father, demonstrating the Father's acceptance of the sacrifice of his Son as the only satisfactory basis for our justification. Now the crucified and resurrected Christ "is at the right hand of God," resting from his finished work, occupying the place of supreme honor, exercising his authority to save and waiting for his final triumph. He "is also interceding for us," for he is our heavenly advocate and high priest.

"Who shall separate us from the love of Christ?" Paul brings forward a sample list of seven adversities and adversaries that might be thought of as coming between us and Christ's love. These are real sufferings—unpleasant, demeaning, painful, hard to bear and challenging to faith. Paul will next respond to his own question with a resounding expression of confidence in Christ.

More Than Conquerors

ROMANS 8:37-39

> ³⁷No, in all these things we are more than conquerors through him who loved us. ³⁸For I am convinced that neither death nor life, neither angels nor demons, neither the present nor the future, nor any powers, ³⁹neither height nor depth, nor anything else in all creation, will be able to separate us from the love of God that is in Christ Jesus our Lord.

Paul knew what he was talking about when he listed numerous afflictions because he had experienced them all, and worse. Perhaps the Roman Christians were also enduring similar trials. Nevertheless, can pain, misery and loss separate Christ's people from his love? No! On the contrary, far from alienating us from him, "in all these things" (even while we are enduring them) Paul dares to claim that "we are more than conquerors." Since Christ proved his love for us by his sufferings, our sufferings cannot possibly separate us from his love.

Paul has asked whether anything will separate us from Christ's love; he now declares that nothing can and so nothing will. He chooses ten items that some might think powerful enough to create a barrier between us and Christ. He mentions them in four pairs, while leaving the remaining two on their own.

"Neither death nor life" presumably alludes to the crisis of death and the calamities of life. "Neither angels nor demons" perhaps includes all cosmic, superhuman agencies, whether good or bad. Since Christ has triumphed over them all, it is certain that they cannot harm us.

The next two pairs refer to time ("neither the present nor the future") and space ("neither height nor depth"), while in between them, on their own, come unspecified "powers." Paul concludes with "nor anything else in all creation," in order to make sure that his inventory is comprehensive and that nothing has been left out. Everything in creation is under the control of God the Creator and of Jesus Christ the Lord.

Paul's previous five questions were not arbitrary. They ask about the kind of God we believe in. Paul's answers affirm that absolutely nothing can frustrate God's purpose (since he is for us) or quench his generosity (since he has not spared his Son) or accuse or condemn his elect (since he has justified them through Christ) or sunder us from his love (since he has revealed it in Christ).

Today we urgently need the assurances Paul offers us, since nothing in our world seems stable. Insecurity is written across all human experience. Christian people are not guaranteed immunity to temptation, tribulation or tragedy, but we are promised victory over them. God's pledge is not that suffering will never afflict us but that it will never separate us from his love. Our confidence is not in our love for him, which is frail, fickle and faltering, but in his love for us, which is steadfast, faithful and persevering.

Romans 8:18-39

....

DISCUSSION GUIDE

OPEN

Theologians sometimes say that we live in the "already but not yet." Christians are already part of God's family, but we are not yet living in the perfect world God designed, nor are we yet perfect physically, mentally or spiritually. What do you long for that is a part of your "not yet"?

STUDY

Read Romans 8:18–39.

1. What examples of present suffering do you see in verses 18-27?

2. How is the future glory described?

3. Verses 24-25 speak of hope. What is the hope that is defined here? In what practical ways can you express this sort of hope?

4. Notice the three uses of the word *groan* in this passage. What does each use of this word suggest about suffering and about hope?

5. Focus on verses 26-27. What do you appreciate about the Holy Spirit's work as it is described here?

6. Focus on verses 28-30. What five actions does God take toward his people? (Define each as accurately as you can.)

7. In view of these actions of God, what encouragement do you find in verse 28?

8. Find five questions in verses 31-39. What is the cumulative impact of these questions?

9. What do these verses reveal about God?

10. How might the love of God, as it is revealed here, help you deal with some of your current pain?

APPLY

1. What signs of a "groaning" creation are particularly painful to you?

2. What signs do you see of your own incompleteness—compared to our future glory?

3. How is God's love nudging you toward that future glory?

Guidelines for Leaders

My grace is sufficient for you.

2 CORINTHIANS 12:9

❦

If leading a small group is something new for you, don't worry. These sessions are designed to flow naturally and be led easily. You may even find that the studies seem to lead themselves!

This study guide is flexible. You can use it with a variety of groups—students, professionals, coworkers, friends, neighborhood or church groups. Each study takes forty-five to sixty minutes in a group setting.

You don't need to be an expert on the Bible or a trained teacher to lead a small group. These guides are designed to facilitate a group's discussion, not a leader's presentation. Guiding group members to discover together what the Bible has to say and to listen together for God's guidance will help them remember much more than a lecture would.

There are some important facts to know about group dynamics and encouraging discussion. The suggestions that follow should equip you to effectively and enjoyably fulfill your role as leader.

PREPARING FOR THE STUDY

1. Ask God to help you understand and apply the passage in your own life. Unless this happens, you will not be prepared to lead others. Pray too for the various members of the group. Ask God to open your hearts to the message of his Word and motivate you to action.

2. Read the introduction to the entire guide to get an overview of the topics that will be explored. *The Message of Romans* will give you more detailed information on the text. This can help you deal with answers to tough questions about the text and its context that could come up in discussion.

3. As you begin each study, read and reread the assigned Bible passage to familiarize yourself with it.

4. Carefully work through each question in the study. Spend time in meditation and reflection as you consider how to respond.

5. Write your thoughts and responses. This will help you to express your understanding of the passage clearly.

6. It may help to have a Bible dictionary handy. Use it to look up any unfamiliar words, names or places.

7. Reflect seriously on how you need to apply the Scripture to your life. Remember that the group members will follow

your lead in responding to the studies. They will not go any deeper than you do.

LEADING THE STUDY

1. At the beginning of your first time together, explain that these studies are meant to be discussions, not lectures. Encourage the members of the group to participate. However, do not put pressure on those who may be hesitant to speak—especially during the first few sessions.

2. Be sure that everyone in your group has a book. Encourage the group to prepare beforehand for each discussion by reading the introduction to the book and the readings for each section.

3. Begin each study on time. Open with prayer, asking God to help the group to understand and apply the passage.

4. Discuss the "Open" question before the Bible passage is read. The "Open" question introduces the theme of the study and helps group members begin to open up, and can reveal where our thoughts and feelings need to be transformed by Scripture. Reading the passage first could tend to color the honest reactions people might otherwise give—because they are, of course, supposed to think the way the Bible does. Encourage as many members as possible to respond to the "Open" question, and be ready to get the discussion going with your own response.

5. Have a group member read aloud the passage to be studied as indicated in the guide.

6. The study questions are designed to be read aloud just as they are written. You may, however, prefer to express them in your own words. There may be times when it is appropriate to deviate from the discussion guide. For example, a question may have already been answered. If so, move on to the next question. Or someone may raise an important question not covered in the guide. Take time to discuss it, but try to keep the group from going off on tangents.

7. Avoid answering your own questions. An eager group quickly becomes passive and silent if members think the leader will do most of the talking. If necessary, repeat or rephrase the question until it is clearly understood, or refer to the commentary woven into the guide to clarify the context or meaning.

8. Don't be afraid of silence in response to the discussion questions. People may need time to think about the question before formulating their answers.

9. Don't be content with just one answer. Ask, "What do the rest of you think?" or "Anything else?" until several people have given answers to the question.

10. Try to be affirming whenever possible. Affirm participation. Never reject an answer; if it is clearly off-base, ask, "Which verse led you to that conclusion?" or again, "What do the rest of you think?"

11. Don't expect every answer to be addressed to you, even though this will probably happen at first. As group members

become more at ease, they will begin to truly interact with each other. This is one sign of healthy discussion.

12. Don't be afraid of controversy. It can be very stimulating. If you don't resolve an issue completely, don't be frustrated. Explain that the group will move on and God may enlighten all of you in later sessions.

13. Periodically summarize what the group has said about the passage. This helps to draw together the various ideas mentioned and gives continuity to the study. But don't preach.

14. Conclude your time together with prayer, asking for God's help in following through on the applications you've identified.

15. End on time.

Many more suggestions and helps for studying a passage or guiding discussion can be found in *How to Lead a LifeGuide Bible Study* and *The Big Book on Small Groups* (both from InterVarsity Press).

Reading the Bible with John Stott

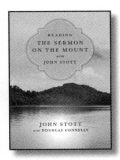

Reading the Sermon on the Mount with John Stott
978-0-8308-3193-7

Reading Romans with John Stott, volume 1
978-0-8308-3191-3

Reading Romans with John Stott, volume 2
978-0-8308-3192-0

ALSO AVAILABLE

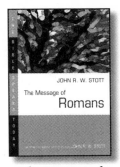

The Message of Romans
978-0-8308-1246-2

FOR TWO THOUSAND YEARS, Paul's letter to the Romans has been a touchstone for all who want to understand the power of the gospel and the righteousness of God revealed from heaven. The truth in Romans transforms our thinking and convicts our hearts as we discover the power of the gospel for every area of our life and our world.

In this volume, the first half of John Stott's *The Message of Romans* is offered as brief readings suitable for daily use. Including ten weekly studies that take us passage by passage through Romans 1–8, this book allows readers to enjoy the riches of Stott's writings in a new, easy-to-use format. The remainder of Romans is presented in the companion to this volume.

"These sensitively edited extracts from Stott's writings will not only introduce new readers to the riches of his biblical exposition (and make them hungry for more), but will surely also introduce them to riches of God's Word they had not seen before."
CHRISTOPHER J. H. WRIGHT
international ministries director, Langham Partnership

"No one I have known has loved, preached, taught and lived the Bible any more than John Stott. He often quoted Spurgeon's comment that we should seek for our very blood to become 'Bibline'; so seriously should we soak in Scripture in order to know and live it. This new series will give us daily help in just such living."
MARK LABBERTON
president, Fuller Theological Seminary, author of *Called*

JOHN STOTT (1921–2011) was known worldwide as a preacher, evangelist and communicator of Scripture. His best-selling books are *Basic Christianity* and *The Cross of Christ*, along with his eight volumes in The Bible Speaks Today series of New Testament expositions. Stott was honored by *Time* magazine in 2005 as one of the "100 Most Influential People in the World."

DALE AND SANDY LARSEN are writers living in Rochester, Minnesota. Together they have written more than thirty books and Bible studies, including *Growing Older and Wiser*.

ISBN 978-0-8308-3191-3

RELIGION / Christian Life / Devotional

IVP Connect
Exploring Faith. Shaping Lives.   www.ivpress.com

9 780830 831913